George MacDonald

Selections from His Greatest Works

George MacDonald Novels
Published by Victor Books

A Quiet Neighborhood
The Seaboard Parish
The Vicar's Daughter
The Last Castle
The Prodigal Apprentice
On Tangled Paths
The Elect Lady
Home Again
The Boyhood of Ranald Bannerman
The Genius of Willie MacMichael
The Wanderings of Clare Skymer
The Shopkeeper's Daughter
Heather and Snow

GEORGE MACDONALD

SELECTIONS FROM HIS GREATEST WORKS

Edited by
David L. Neuhouser

VICTOR BOOKS®

A DIVISION OF SCRIPTURE PRESS PUBLICATIONS INC.
USA CANADA ENGLAND

Library of Congress Cataloging-in-Publication Data

MacDonald, George, 1824-1905.
   [Selections. 1990]
   George MacDonald : selections from his greatest works /
edited by David L. Neuhouser.
      p.   cm.
   Includes bibliographical references.
   ISBN 0-89693-788-7
   1. MacDonald, George, 1824-1905—Quotations. 2. Quo-
tations, English. I. Neuhouser, David L. II. Title.
   PR4966.N48 1990
   828'.802—dc20   89-77802
                                                CIP

1 2 3 4 5 6 7 8 9 10 Printing / Year 94   93   92   91   90

CONTENTS

FOREWORD

I am very heartened by the renewed interest in the writings of George MacDonald. Years ago, as a result of reading tributes made by C.S. Lewis to the contribution made in his thinking by one George MacDonald, I decided to go to the source. Most of us who read Lewis, MacDonald, and Charles Williams probably connected up in the same way. Now we have a much increased fellowship of people with whom to share our discoveries and excitement. For me, getting permission to question certain long-held ideas was a breath of fresh air. Faith no longer was an absence of doubt, which I couldn't control anyway, but in MacDonald suddenly doubt, honestly pursued, became the raw material of new confidence and faith. I was greatly relieved that faith did not involve intellectual *kamikaze*. Again, through MacDonald, I learned that obedience, even in the face of questions, produces faith as a by-product. Now this practice is second nature but at its discovery it was revolutionary. David Neuhouser has provided us with an anthology and an exposure to MacDonald's central ideas that will be an enrichment to new readers and a source of joy and reaffirmation to old MacDonald friends. We welcome this exposure to the years of study and research that Neuhouser has devoted to his love of MacDonald.

Jay Kesler, President, Taylor University

INTRODUCTION

About twenty years ago, thanks to C.S. Lewis, I began searching through used bookstores for copies of George MacDonald's novels. These novéls had long been out of print, but were full of "spiritual knowledge," to use Lewis' description. Fortunately, I was able to acquire most of them before the prices were driven up because of so many other people following Lewis' advice. In a letter to his friend Arthur Greeves (Dec. 10, 1942), Lewis said, "I have introduced such a lot of people to MacDonald this year: in nearly every case with success." Through his books he has introduced many more people to MacDonald. For example, in a question and answer session after one of her lectures, Madeleine L'Engle said that the biggest influence Lewis had on her writing was to introduce her to the writings of George MacDonald.

MacDonald's novels and fairy tales were quite popular, both in England and America when they were first published. Some of his fairy tales have maintained their popularity. However, his novels were out of print for several decades, partly because of their outspoken Christian teaching. His books influenced the ideas of many Christians of his day. In addition to Lewis and L'Engle, other famous authors have been influenced by MacDonald; for example, G.K. Chesterton, W.H. Auden, and J.R.R. Tolkien.

In the process of my reading and rereading the novels, I have marked many passages for future reference and now I would like to share some of these. Providentially (I believe), his novels are now available in edited form and the complete novels and collections of sermons are becoming available in limited editions. His fairy tales are also readily available in many forms. However, there are many gems in the original novels which get cut in the editing process and most people do not have access to the unedited books. Then there are people who just aren't interested in reading novels or fairy tales but would be interested in the Christian teachings. So I believe that a collection of MacDonald quotations would introduce many new people to this great Christian teacher.

Lewis recognized that MacDonald's novels have many faults as novels mainly because he had to turn them out so fast in order to make enough money to support a large family (eleven children). Still, Lewis enjoyed many things about them; the fairy-tale like quality of some parts, the melodrama, the ideal characters, and the direct preaching. Of MacDonald's characters, he said they are "highly idealized. Yet somehow they convince me. Or if they don't quite convince me as real people, they differ from most ideal characters in this, that I wish they *were* real" (Jan. 17, 1931 letter to Greeves). In *Sir Gibbie,* MacDonald defends his presentation of ideal characters. He said, "I insist that what ought to be presented . . . is the common good uncommonly developed, and that not because of its rarity, but because it is truer to humanity . . . the representation of a man trying to be merely as noble as is absolutely essential to his being."

George MacDonald was born December 10, 1824 in Huntly, Scotland. He was ordained as a pastor in the Congregational Church and held a pastorate in Arundel for a few years. He lost that position and was not able to obtain another pastorate because of some doctrinal differences with his deacons. However, he never lost his call to preach. He used novels as his pulpit. He preferred writing poetry and fairy tales to novels, but novels sold better. He found that through his novels he could preach to more people than he would have been able to do in any pastorate, and he could support his growing family. He defended his preaching in his books by saying that he had a Master to serve.

What Lewis said about the novel *What's Mine's Mine* he probably believed was true about MacDonald's other novels as well. He said that "it is good not despite, but because of, its preaching—or rather (preaching is a bad word) its spiritual knowledge. So many clever writers strike one as quite childish after MacDonald: they seem not even to have begun to understand so many things" (Feb. 23, 1931 letter to Greeves). In another letter (August 31, 1930), "I know nothing that gives me such a feeling of spiritual healing, of being washed, as to read G. MacDonald."

Although his novels were MacDonald's chief outlet for his preaching and supplied a great part of his income, he was involved in many other activities. He never had a regular pastorate after Arundel; however, he continued to preach wherever and whenever he could. He taught natural science and mathematics as well as English literature at various colleges in Manchester and London. As a lecturer, chiefly on English literature, he was quite popular. In 1872, he had a very successful American lecture tour. His Robert Burns lectures were the most popular. Also, among his many varied works are collections of poems, sermons, and literary essays.

Almost everything he ever wrote contains Christian teaching. Even in his essays on literature, we find gems of spiritual insight. At first, I meant to include in this anthology only selections from the novels, but decided that that was too limiting. By including material from fairy tales (both children's and adult's), sermons, essays, and poetry, we are able to explore more fully MacDonald's understanding of Christianity. Besides, for those readers who are not familiar with MacDonald or are only familiar with his novels, this will be an introduction to the rest of MacDonald's writing. For example, his poems are not readily available, so I have included a sample of his poetry.

MacDonald emphasized God's love (tough love), obedience, and humility. My favorite quotation of his is, "God is easy to please, but hard to satisfy." That is, He will never be satisfied with us until we are perfect, but He is pleased with our progress along the way. But even though He may be pleased with our small steps, that won't keep Him from doing whatever is necessary, even if it is painful, to help us move toward that "mature manhood, to the measure of the stature of the fullness of Christ." Our part in that process is to obey. Even the smallest step of obedience leads to spiritual growth and knowledge.

In this collection, I have chosen eleven topics which MacDonald emphasized. I have tried to pick enough quotations to show the range and depth of MacDonald's thoughts on each. In reading this anthology you will hear parts of conversations and get glimpses of incidents. I believe that you will be able to understand the message without knowing the entire plot of the novel from which it is taken. On the other hand, I make no secret of the fact that I hope you get so intrigued that you will want to read the novels themselves, the originals if you can get them, or if not, then the edited forms.

After each quotation, within parentheses, will be given the page numbers and title abbreviations. If an asterisk (*) is there, it means that Scottish dialect has been translated into English. At the beginning of the anthology is a key to the title abbreviations. Sometimes, at the beginning of a quotation, again within parentheses, I have given the setting in order to better understand the quotation. Except for the changes from Scottish dialect into English, the only changes I have made is to capitalize pronouns that refer to God, and that is for increased clarity.

The first eleven chapters are topical. The last chapter is poetry. Each quotation is numbered and these numbers are used in a subject index. The index includes nearly a hundred entries including the chapter titles since quotations in one chapter may well include discussion of another chapter's topic. MacDonald hardly ever has a sentence, and even more rarely, a paragraph on only one topic. He is constantly relating things such as, faith and imagination or love, obedience, and knowledge. This is what makes his writing so rich.

This book may be used in many ways. One way would be the study of topics by using either chapter headings or index entries. Since the index is not complete, I would encourage the reader to enlarge and personalize it by reading the entire collection and adding topics of personal interest or adding more quotation numbers to present entries. Another way of using this book would be to read one or more entries daily as part of a devotional period.

My recommended approach is to read it through to get a fuller understanding of MacDonald's thoughts. Any passage, by itself, could be misunderstood. But other passages on the same subject qualify, amplify, and clarify so that the thoughtful reader should be able to understand the subtlety and depth of MacDonald's thinking. Most of the entries are short, a few longer selections (usually from a novel) are included.

One bit of advice about the use of the index: if a topic you are interested in is not listed, try a synonym (e.g., for "wrath," look under "anger") or an antonym (e.g., for "weakness," look under "strength").

My understanding of MacDonald has been helped by conversations with my wife Ruth, and with my children, students, and friends. I thank them all. Special thanks also go to Taylor University for giving me the opportunity to teach C.S. Lewis/George MacDonald seminars; to Dr. Ed Brown, who helped me build my MacDonald collection; to Dan and Elizabeth Hamilton, for encouragement in many ways; to Carole Streeter and Barbara Williams for many helpful suggestions; and to Ruth Neuhouser, Carol Stocksdale, and especially Margaret Neideck, for their typing and proofreading skills.

ABBREVIATIONS

This collection has been compiled from the following editions of George MacDonald's works:

AB   *At the Back of the North Wind,* Akron, Ohio: Saalfield Publishing Co., 1927.

AF   *Alec Forbes of Howglen,* London: Hurst and Blackett, Publishers, n.d.

AN   *Annals of a Quiet Neighborhood,* Philadelphia: David McKay, Publisher, n.d.

DE   *David Elginbrod,* Boston: Loring, Publisher, n.d.

DG   *Donal Grant,* Boston: Lothrop Publishing Co., 1883.

DO   *Dish of Orts,* London: Edwin Dalton, 1908.

DS   *Diary of an Old Soul,* Minneapolis: Augsburg Publishing House, 1975.

E   *The Elect Lady,* London: Kegan Paul, Trench, Trubner and Co., Ltd., n.d.

EA   *England's Antiphon,* New York: MacMillan and Co., 1890.

FS   *The Flight of the Shadow,* San Francisco: Harper and Row, Publishers, 1983.

GC   *Guild Court,* Philadelphia: David McKay, Publisher, n.d.

GK   *The Golden Key and Other Stories,* Elgin, Illinois: Scripture Union, 1979.

GP   *Gutta Percha Willie: the Working Genius,* London: Blackie and Son Limited, n.d.

GW   *God's Word to His Children,* New York: Funk and Wagnalls, 1887.

HA   *Home Again,* London: Kegan Paul, Trench, Trubner and Co., Ltd., 1900.

HG   *Hope of the Gospel,* London: Ward, Lock, Bowden

and Co., 1892.

HS   *Heather and Snow,* London: Chatto and Windus, 1915.

L   *Lilith,* Grand Rapids, Michigan: Eerdman's, 1981.

M   *Malcolm,* Philadelphia: David McKay, Publisher, n.d.

ML   *The Marquis of Lossie,* London: Kegan Paul, Trench, Trubner and Co., Ltd., n.d.

MM   *Mary Marston,* New York: George Routledge and Sons, Limited, n.d.

MOL   *The Miracles of Our Lord,* London: Strahan and Co., Publishers, 1870.

P   *The Portent,* San Francisco: Harper and Row, Publishers, 1979.

PI   *Poetical Works,* Volume I, London: Chatto and Windus, 1911.

PII   *Poetical Works,* Volume II, London: Chatto and Windus, 1911.

PC   *The Princess and Curdie,* Elgin, Illinois: Scripture Union, 1979.

PF   *Paul Faber, Surgeon,* Philadelphia: David McKay, Publisher, n.d.

PG   *The Princess and the Goblin,* Elgin, Illinois: Scripture Union, 1979.

PH   *Phantastes,* Grand Rapids, Michigan: Eerdmans, 1981.

RB   *Ranald Bannerman's Boyhood,* Philadelphia: J.B. Lippencott Company, 1890.

RF   *Robert Falconer,* New York: George Routledge and Sons, Limited, n.d.

RS   *A Rough Shaking,* London: Blackie and Son, Limited, 1890.

SI   *Unspoken Sermons (Series One),* London: Alexander Strahan, 1867.

SII   *Unspoken Sermons (Series Two),* London: Longmans, Green, and Co., 1895.

SIII *Unspoken Sermons (Series Three),* London: Longmans, Green, and Co., 1891.

SF   *Salted with Fire,* London: Hurst and Blackett, Limited, n.d.

SG   *Sir Gibbie,* London: J.M. Dent and Sons, Limited, 1911.

SGM   *Saint George and Saint Michael,* Philadelphia: David McKay, Publisher, n.d.

SP   *The Seaboard Parish,* Philadelphia: David McKay, Publisher, n.d.

TB   *There and Back,* Boston: D. Lothrop Co., 1891.

TW   *Thomas Wingfold, Curate,* London: Kegan Paul, Trench, Trubner and Co., Ltd., 1906.

V   *The Vicar's Daughter,* London: Sampson Low, Marston, Searle, and Rivington, 1881.

WC   *Wilfred Cumbermede,* Chicago: Belford, Clarke and Co., 1881.

WM   *What's Mine's Mine,* London: Kegan Paul, Trench, Trubner and Co., Ltd., 1900.

WW   *Weighed and Wanting,* Boston: D. Lothrop Co., 1893.

The source of each citation is indicated by a letter-number code following each excerpt. The letter represents the corresponding book from the key above. The number is the book's page number.

ONE

 GOD

1. "What is Christianity, then?"
   "God in Christ, and Christ in man."

(TW, 78)

2. Jesus Christ is the *only* likeness of the living Father.

(SIII, 44)

3. Jesus alone knows the Father and can reveal Him.

(SG, 153)

4. The one use of the Bible is to make us look at Jesus, that through Him we might know His Father and our Father, His God and our God. Till we thus know Him, let us hold the Bible dear as the moon of our darkness, by which we travel towards the east; not dear as the sun whence her light cometh, and towards which we haste, that, walking in the sun Himself, we may no more need the mirror that reflects His absent brightness.

(SI, 55)

5. The true heart goes to the blessed Book, not as an idolater, but as a disciple; not to worship the Book, but to

learn the will of Him who made the Book, and who has made His spirit to understand the Book.

(GW, 113)

6. I believe that there is nothing good for me or for any man but God, and more and more of God, and that alone through knowing Christ can we come nigh to Him.

(SIII, 154)

7. I believe in Jesus Christ, the eternal Son of God, my elder brother, my Lord and Master; I believe that He has a right to my absolute obedience whereinsoever I know or shall come to know His will; that to obey Him is to ascent the pinnacle of my being; that not to obey Him would be to deny Him.

(SIII, 153)

8. I believe that He died that I might die like Him—die to any ruling power in me but the will of God—live ready to be nailed to the cross as He was, if God will it.

(SIII, 153)

9. I believe that He is my Saviour from myself, and from all that has come of loving myself, from all that God does not love, and would not have me love—all that is not worth loving; that He died that the justice, the mercy of God, might have its way with me, making me just as God is just, merciful as He is merciful, perfect as my Father in Heaven is perfect.

(SIII, 153)

10. I believe and pray that He will give me what punishment I need to set me right, or keep me from going wrong. I believe that He died to deliver me from all meanness, all pretence, all falseness, all unfairness, all poverty of spirit, all cowardice, all fear, all anxiety, all forms of self-love, all trust or hope in possession; to make me merry as a child, the child of our Father in heaven, loving nothing but what is

lovely, desiring nothing I should be ashamed to let the universe of God see me desire.

(SIII, 153–54)

11. To arouse the hope that there may be a God with a heart like our own is more for the humanity in us than to produce the absolute conviction that there is a being who made the heaven and the earth and the sea and the fountains of waters. Jesus is the express image of God's substance, and in Him we know the heart of God.

(MOL, 197)

12. The worst heresy, next to that of dividing religion and righteousness, is to divide the Father from the Son—in thought or feeling or action or intent; to represent the Son as doing that which the Father does not Himself do. Jesus did nothing but what the Father did and does.

(SII, 143)

13. Christ is the way out, and the way in; the way from slavery, conscious or unconscious, into liberty; the way from the unhomeliness of things to the home we desire but do not know; the way from the stormy skirts of the Father's garments to the peace of His bosom. To picture Him, we need not only endless figures, but sometimes quite opposing figures: He is not only the door of the sheepfold, but the shepherd of the sheep; He is not only the way, but the leader in the way, the rock that followed, and the captain of our salvation.

(SII, 210)

14. We must forsake all our fears and distrusts for Christ. We must receive His teaching heartily, nor let the interpretation of it attributed to His apostles make us turn aside from it. I say interpretation attributed to them; for what they teach is never against what Christ taught, though very often the exposition of it is—and that from no fault in the apostles, but from the grievous fault of those who would

understand, and even explain, rather than obey.

(SII, 251)

15. He brothers us. He takes us to the knees of the Father, beholding whose face we grow sons indeed. Never could we have known the heart of the Father, never felt it possible to love Him as sons, but for Him who cast Himself into the gulf that yawned between us.

(SII, 129)

16. The Saviour of whom she spoke so often, and evidently thought so much, was in a great measure a being of her fancy—so much so that she manifested no desire to find out what the Christ was who had spent three and thirty years in making a revelation of Himself to the world. The knowledge she had about Him was not even at the second hand but at many removes. She did not study His words or His actions to learn His thoughts or His meanings; but lived in a dreamland of her own which could be interesting only to the dreamer. Now if we are going to come to God through Christ, it must surely be by knowing Christ; it must be through the knowledge of Christ that the Spirit of the Father mainly works in the members of His body; and it seemed to me she did not take the trouble to "know Him and the power of His resurrection."

(V, 323–24)

17. God is God to us not that we may say *He is, but that we may know Him;* and when we know Him, then we are with Him, at home, at the heart of the universe, the heir of all things.

(TB, 364)

18. God is not a God that hides, but a God that reveals. . . . That we are in the dark about anything is never because He hides it, but because we are not yet such that He is able to reveal that thing to us.

(SIII, 229)

19. No revelation can be other than partial. If for true revelation a man must be told all the truth, then farewell to revelation.... For what revelation, other than a partial, can the highest spiritual condition receive of the infinite God? But it is not therefore untrue because it is partial.

(SI, 35)

20. Our longing desires can no more exhaust the fulness of the treasures of the Godhead, than our imagination can touch their measure.

(SI, 24)

21. You can find nothing but what the Lord teaches you. If you find what I tell you untrue, it will be in not being enough—in not being grand and free and bounteous enough. To think anything too good to be true is to deny God—to say the untrue is better than the true.... It will be something better and better, lovelier and lovelier that Christ will teach you.

(DG, 445)

22. It is only as they help us toward God, that our opinions are worth a straw; and every necessary change in them must be to more truth, to greater uplifting power. Lord, change me as Thou wilt, only do not send me away.

(DO, 295)

23. The still small voice is ever reminding us that the Lord is neither in the earthquake nor the wind nor the fire; but in the lowly heart that finds Him everywhere.

(MOL, 259)

24. Then ... broke the heavenliest smile she had every seen ... a smile that was a clearer revelation of God than ten thousand books about Him.

(RS, 61)

25. [Paul] had seen Jesus with his bodily eyes, I think, but he had not seen Him with those alone; he had seen ... Him with the real eyes, the eyes that do not see except they understand; and the sight of Him had uplifted his whole nature—first his pure will for righteousness, and then his hoping imagination; and out of these, in the knowledge of Jesus, he spoke.

(HG, 202)

26. The reality of Christ's nature is not to be proved by argument. He must be beheld.

(DO, 206)

27. Of all teachings that which presents a far distant God is the nearest to absurdity. Either there is none, or He is nearer to every one of us than our nearest consciousness of self. An unapproachable divinity is the veriest of monsters, the most horrible of human imaginations.

(SG, 166)

28. Friend, you are close to God, infinitely closer than your imagination can represent to you; and if you do not know it, you are in the very essence a poor, foolish thing— whom God has not forgotten, though.

(GW, 4)

29. Think, brothers, think, sisters, we walk in the air of an eternal fatherhood. Every uplifting of the heart is a looking up to the Father. Graciousness and truth are around, above, beneath us, yea, *in* us.

(SI, 186)

30. The darkness knows neither the light nor itself; only the light knows itself and the darkness also. None but God hates evil and understands it.

(L, 206)

31. The Lord never does the next best. The thing He does is always better than the thing He does not.

(E, 324)

32. All misery is *God unknown.*

(HA, 192)

33. Life is no series of chances with a few providences sprinkled between to keep up a justly failing belief, but one providence of God....

(SI, 26)

34. The next hour, the next moment, is as much beyond our grasp and as much in God's care, as that a hundred years away. Care for the next minute is just as foolish as care for the morrow, or for a day in the next thousand years—in neither can we do anything, in both God is doing everything. Those claims only of the morrow which have to be prepared to-day are of the duty of to-day; the moment which coincides with work to be done, is the moment to be minded; the next is nowhere till God has made it.

(SII, 46)

35. Certain of his formerly petted doctrines he now threw away as worse than rubbish; others he dropped with indifference, of some it was as if the angels picked his pocket without his knowing it, or ever missing them; and still he found, whatever so-called doctrine he parted with, that the one glowing truth which had lain at the heart of it, buried, mired, obscured, not only remained with him, but shone out fresh, restored to itself by the loss of the clay-lump of worldly figures and phrases, in which the human intellect had enclosed it. His faith was elevated, and so confirmed.

(PF, 347)

36. The possibility had not yet dawned upon her that there could be anything in the New Testament but those doctrines against which the best in [her son] revolted. She

little suspected the glory of sky and earth and sea eternal that would one day burst upon her! That she would one day see God not only good but infinitely better than she had dared to think Him, fearing to image Him better than He was! Mortal, she dreaded being more just than God, more pure than her maker!

(WM, 113)

37. If God punish sin, it must be merciful to punish sin; and if God forgive sin, it must be just to forgive sin.

(SIII, 119)

38. If it be said by any that God does a thing, and the thing seems to me unjust, then either I do not know what the thing is, or God does not do it.

(SIII, 118)

39. I believe that justice and mercy are simply one and the same thing; without justice to the full there can be no mercy, and without mercy to the full there can be no justice; that such is the mercy of God that He will hold His children in the consuming fire of His distance until they pay the uttermost farthing, until they drop the purse of selfishness with all the dross that is in it, and rush home to the Father and the Son, and the many brethren—rush inside the centre of the life-giving fire whose outer circles burn.

(SIII, 155)

40. Because He is just, we are capable of knowing justice; it is because He is just, that we have the idea of justice so deeply imbedded in us.

(SIII, 110)

41. There is *no* opposition, *no* strife whatever, between mercy and justice. Those who say justice means the punishing of sin, and mercy the not punishing of sin, and attribute both to God, would make a schism in the very idea of God.

(SIII, 114)

42. Where there is no ground to believe that God does a thing except that men who would explain God have believed and taught it, he is not a true man who accepts men against his own conscience of God. I acknowledge no authority calling upon me to believe a thing of God, which I could not be a man and believe right in my fellowman.

(SIII, 117)

43. If you say, That may be right of God to do which it would not be right of man to do, I answer, Yes, because the relation of the Maker to His creatures is very different from the relation of one of those creatures to another, and He has therefore duties toward His creatures requiring of Him what no man would have the right to do to his fellowman; but He can have no duty that is not both just and merciful.

(SIII, 117–18)

44. ... it was not this and that fault He had come to set right, but the primary evil of life without God, the root of all evils, from hatred to discourtesy.

(SII, 46)

45. He is against sin: in so far as, and while, they and sin are one, He is against them—against their desires, their aims, their fears, and their hopes; and thus He is altogether and always *for them*.

(SI, 38)

46. (A conversation fragment between the rector and his curate.)
   "God only knows whether I haven't been breaking

every one of the commandments I used to read to them every Sunday."

"But God does know, sir," said the curate, with even more than his usual respect in his tone, "and that is well, for otherwise we might go on breaking them forever."

(PF, 67)

47. I believe that no man is ever condemned for any sin except one—that he will not leave his sins and come out of them, and be the child of Him who is his Father.

(SIII, 154–55)

48. He has not two thoughts about us. With Him all is simplicity of purpose and meaning and effort and end— namely, that we should be as He is, think the same thoughts, mean the same things, possess the same blessedness.

(SI, 22)

49. The gift of the Spirit of God to make you think as God thinks, feel as God feels, judge as God judges, is just the one thing that is promised.

(DO, 311)

50. Sisters, brothers, we cannot meet save in God.

(WW, 213)

51. What father is not pleased with the first tottering attempt of his little one to walk? What father would be satisfied with anything but the manly step of the full-grown son?

(SII, 10–11)

52. We do our brother, our sister, grievous wrong, every time that, in our selfish justice, we forget the excuse that mitigates the blame. That God never does, for it would be to disregard the truth. As He will never admit a false excuse, so will He never neglect a true one. It may be He makes excuses which the sinner dares not think of; while

the most specious of false ones shrivel into ashes before
Him. A man is bound to think of all just excuse for his
offender, for less than the righteousness of God will not
serve his turn.

(PF, 266)

53. Sometimes a thunderbolt, as men call it, will shoot
from a clear sky; and sometimes, into the midst of a peaceful family, or a yet quieter individuality, without warning of
gathered storm above or slightest tremble of earthquake
beneath, will fall a terrible fact, and from the moment everything is changed. That family or that life is no more what
it was—probably never more can be what it was. Better it
ought to be, worse it may be—which, depends upon itself.
But its spiritual weather is altered. The air is thick with
cloud, and cannot weep itself clear. There may come a
gorgeous sunset, though.

(TW, 99)

54. To the man who believes in the Son of God, poetry
returns in a mighty wave; history unrolls itself in harmony;
science shows crowned with its own aureole of holiness.
There is no enlivener of the imagination, no enabler of the
judgment, no strengthener of the intellect, to compare with
the belief in a live Ideal, at the heart of all personality, as of
every law.

(DO, 75)

55. The light of our life, our sole, eternal, and infinite joy,
is simply God—God—God—nothing but God, and all His
creatures in Him.

(SIII, 221)

56. And the man has begun to be strong who has begun to
know that, separated from life essential, that is God, he is
weakness itself, but of strength inexhaustible if he be one
with his origin.

(DG, 445)

57. ... to see God and to love Him are one.

(HG, 162)

58. ... let us have grace to serve the Consuming Fire, our God, with divine fear; not with the fear that cringes and craves, but with the bowing down of all thoughts, all delights, all loves before Him who is the life of them all, and will have them all pure.

(SI, 30)

59. He has set before us a way that we may turn, and, of our own free will, run back to Him, embrace the Father's knees, and be lifted to the Father's heart.

(GW, 28)

60. The kingdom of heaven is not come, even when God's will is our law: it is come when God's will is our will. While God's will is our law, we are but a kind of noble slaves: when His will is our will, we are free children. Nothing in nature is free enough to be a symbol for the state of those who act immediately from the essence of their hidden life, and the recognition of God's will as that essence.

(DE, 374–75)

61. "Do you think God cares to have me do His will? Is it anything to Him?"

"I am sure of it. Why did He make you else? But it is not for the sake of being obeyed that He cares for it, but for the sake of serving you and making you blessed with His blessedness. He does not care about Himself, but about you."

(DE, 408)

62. I believe that to be the disciple of Christ is the end of being; that to persuade men to be His disciples is the end of teaching.

(SIII, 156)

63. I believe that to him who obeys, and thus opens the doors of his heart to receive the eternal gift, God gives the Spirit of His Son, the Spirit of Himself, to be in him, and lead him to the understanding of all truth; that the true disciple shall thus always know what he ought to do, though not necessarily what another ought to do; that the Spirit of the Father and the Son enlightens by teaching righteousness.

(SIII, 155)

64. "O my children!" I said, "if the world could but be brought to believe—the world did I say?—if the best men in the world could only see, as God sees it, that service is in itself the noblest exercise of human powers; if they could see that God is the hardest worker of all, and that His nobility are those who do the most service, surely it would alter the whole aspect of the church. Menial offices, for instance, would soon cease to be talked of with that contempt which shows that there is no true recognition of the fact that the same principle runs through the highest duty and the lowest—that the lowest work which God gives a man to do must be in its nature noble, as certainly noble as the highest. This would destroy condescension which is the rudeness, yes, impertinence of the higher, as it would destroy insolence, which is the rudeness of the lower."

(SP, 78–79)

65. Church or chapel is *not* the place for divine service. It is a place of prayer, a place of praise, a place to feed upon good things, a place to learn of God, as what place is not? It is a place to look in the eyes of your neighbour, and love God along with him. But the world in which you move, the place of your living and loving and labour, not the church you go to on your holiday, is the place of divine service. Serve your neighbour, and you serve Him.

(SIII, 228)

66. For even the best men in the Church . . . were worldly enough to judge the degree of heavenly favour shown them,

not by the love they bore to the truth and to each other, not by the purity of their collective acts and the prevalence of a high standard of morality in the individual . . . but, in a great degree, by the success which attended the preaching of their pastor, in adding to their . . . congregation.

(AF, 312)

67. To God alone we live or die. Let us fall, as, thank Him, we must, into His hands. Let Him judge us. Posterity may be wiser than we; but posterity is not our judge.

(MOL, 166)

68. God will be fair to you—so fair!—fair with the fairness of a father loving his own—who will have you clean, who will neither spare you any needful shame, nor leave you exposed to any that is not needful.

(SIII, 238)

69. When a man dreams his own dream, he is the sport of his dream; when Another gives it him, the Other is able to fulfill it.

(L, 251)

70. "God is nearer to you than any thought or feeling of yours, Lady Emily. Do not be afraid. if all the evil things in the universe were around us, they could not come inside the ring that He makes around us. He always keeps a place for Himself and His child, into which no other being can enter."

"Oh! how you must love God, Margaret!"

"Indeed, I do love Him, my lady. If ever anything looks beautiful or lovely to me, then I know at once that God is that."

"But, then, what right have we to take the good of that, however true it is, when we are not beautiful ourselves?"

"That only makes God the more beautiful,—in that He will pour out the more of His beauty upon us to make us beautiful. If we care for His glory, we shall be glad to believe all this about Him. But we are too anxious about feeling good ourselves, to rejoice in His perfect goodness. I think we should find that enough, my lady. For, if He be good, are not we His children and sure of having it, not merely feeling it, some day?"

(DE, 237–38)

71. "You seem to make everything clear, and right, and plain. I wish I were you, Margaret."

"If I were you, my lady, I would rather be what God chose to make me than the most glorious creature that I could think of. For to have been thought about,—born in God's thoughts,—and then made by God, is the dearest, grandest, most precious thing in all thinking. Is it not, my lady?"

"It is," said Lady Emily, and was silent.

(DE, 238–39)

72. I wonder how many Christians there are who so thoroughly believe God made them that they can laugh in God's name; who understand that God invented laughter and gave it to His children. . . . The Lord of gladness delights in the laughter of a merry heart.

(MOL, 23)

73. The man had a redeeming sense of humor, though he did not know how to prize it, not believing it a gift of God.

(SG, 15)

74. It is the heart that is not yet sure of its God that is afraid to laugh in His presence.

(SG, 152)

75. Man finds it hard to get what he wants, because he does not want the best; God finds it hard to give, because He would give the best, and man will not take it.

(SII, 142)

76. I believe that God has always done, is always doing His best for every man; that no man is miserable because God is forgetting him; that He is not a God to crouch before, but our Father, to whom the child-heart cries exultant, "Do with me as Thou wilt."

(SIII, 154)

77. (In the following passage, the world is compared to a scaffold. This helps us understand things about the world that would trouble us if we thought it was meant for a permanent dwelling place.)

What if it were not meant to stand, then? What if it were meant only for a temporary assistance in carrying out something finished and lasting, and of unspeakably more importance? Suppose God were building a palace for you, and had set up a scaffold, upon which He wanted you to help Him. Would it be reasonable for you to complain that you didn't find the scaffold at all a comfortable place to live in? Or that it was draughty and cold? This world is that scaffold, and if you were busy carrying stones and mortar for the palace, you would be glad of all the cold to cool the glow of your labor. . . .

But what will all the labor of a workman who does not fall in with the design of the builder come to? Instead of working away at the palace, like men, will you go on tacking bits of matting and old carpet about the corners of the scaffold to keep the wind off, while the same wind keeps tearing them away and scattering them? You keep trying to live in a scaffold, which not all eternity would make a house of. God wants to build you a house whereof the walls shall be *goodness*. You want a house with walls of *comfort*. But God knows that such walls cannot be built—that that kind of stone crumbles away in the foolish workman's hands. He would make you comfortable, but neither is that His first object, nor can it be gained without the first, which is to make you good. He loves you so much that He would infinitely rather have you good and uncomfortable—for then He could take you to His heart as His own children—than comfortable and not good, for then He could not come near you, or give you anything He counted worth having. . . .

It comes to this, that when God would build a palace for Himself to dwell in with His children, He does not want His scaffold so constructed that they shall be able to make a house of it for themselves, and live like apes instead of angels.

(V, 259–61)

78. See every flower straighten its stalk, lift up its neck, and with outstretched head stand expectant: something more than the sun, greater than the light, is coming, is coming—none the less surely coming that it is long upon the road! What matters to-day, or tomorrow, or ten thousand years to Life Himself, to Love Himself! He is coming, is coming, and the necks of all humanity are stretched out to see Him come!

(L, 245)

TWO

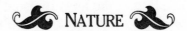 NATURE

79. "I mean by *nature,* then, all that you see and hear and smell and taste and feel of the things round about you. . . . But that is not all. We mean the things themselves only for the sake of what they say to us. As our sense of smell brings us news of fields far off, so those fields, or even the smell only that comes from them, tell us of things, meanings, thoughts, intentions beyond them, and embodied in them."

(WM, 211)

80. Nature is brimful of symbolic and analogical parallels to the goings and comings, the growth and the changes of the highest nature in man. It could not be otherwise. For not only did they issue from the same thought, but the one is made for the other. Nature is an outer garment for man, or a living house, rather, for man to live in.

(MOL, 153–54)

81. To the man of God, all nature will be but changeful reflections of the face of God.

(DO, 256)

82. The heavens and the earth are around us that it may be possible for us to speak of the unseen by the seen; for the outermost husk of creation has correspondence with the deepest things of the Creator.

(SIII, 31)

83. The faces of some flowers lead me back to the heart of God; and, as His child, I hope I feel, in my lowly degree, what He felt when, brooding over them, He said, "They are good;" that is, "They are what I mean."

(SIII, 251)

84. "All about us, in earth and air, wherever eye or ear can reach there is a power ever breathing itself forth in sighs, now in a daisy, now in a wind-waft, a cloud, a sunset; a power that holds constant and sweetest relation with the dark and silent world within us; that the same God who is in us, and upon whose tree we are the buds, if not yet the flowers, also is all about us—inside, the Spirit; outside, the Word. And the two are ever trying to meet in us; and when they meet, then the sign without, and the longing within, become one in light, and the man no more walketh in darkness, but knoweth whither he goeth."

(TW, 415–16)

85. Whether indeed the heavenly bodies *teach* [us the nature of God], or whether we should read divinity worthy of the name in them at all, without the human revelation which healed men, I doubt much. That divinity is there— *Yes:* that we could read it there without having seen the face of the Son of Man first, I think—*No.* . . . power and order, although of God, and preparing the way for Him, are not His revealers unto men. No doubt King David compares the perfection of God's law to the glory of the heavens, but he did not learn that perfection from the heavens, but from the law itself, revealed in his own heart through the life-teaching of God. When he had learned it he saw that the heavens were like it.

To unveil God, only manhood like our own will serve. And He has taken the form of man that He might reveal the manhood in Him from awful eternity.

(EA, 279)

86. He lay gazing up into the depth of the sky, rendered deeper and bluer by the masses of white cloud that hung almost motionless below it until he felt a kind of bodily fear lest he should fall off the face of the round earth into the abyss. A gentle wind, laden with pine odors from the sun-heated trees behind him, flapped its light wing in his face: the humanity of the world smote his heart; the great sky towered up over him, and its divinity entered his soul; a strange longing after something "he knew not nor could name" awoke within him, followed by the pang of a sudden fear that there was no such thing as that which he sought, that it was all a fancy of his own spirit. . . .

Strange as it may sound to those who have never thought of such things save in connection with Sundays and Bibles and churches and sermons, that which was now working in Falconer's mind was the first dull and faint movement of the greatest need that the human heart possesses,—the need of the God-man. There must be truth in the scent of that pinewood: someone must mean it. There must be a glory in those heavens that depends not upon our imagination: some power greater than they must dwell in them. Some spirit must move in that wind that haunts us with a kind of human sorrow; some soul must look up to us from the eye of that flower. It must be something human, else not to us divine.

(RF, 142)

87. In whatever way it may be accounted for, of one thing we may be sure, that this feeling is no cheat; for there is no cheating in nature and the simple unsought feelings of the soul. There must be a truth involved in it, though we may but in part lay hold of the meaning.

(PH, 66–67)

88. They did not know nature: in the school to which they had gone they patronized instead of revering her. She wrought upon them nevertheless after her own fashion with her children unheedful whether they knew what she was about or not. The mere space, the mere height from which they looked, the rarity of the air, the soft aspiration of earth towards heaven, made them all more of children.

(WM, 11)

89. Think for a moment what would be our idea of greatness, of God, of infinitude, of aspiration, if, instead of a blue, far withdrawn, light-spangled firmament, we were born and reared under a flat white ceiling! I would not be supposed to depreciate the labours of science, but I say its discoveries are unspeakably less precious than the merest gifts of Nature, those which, from morning to night, we take unthinking from her hands.

(SII, 197)

90. "Look up," he said, "and tell me what you see.—What is the shape over us?"

"It is a vault," replied Christina.

"A dome—is it not?" said Mercy.

"Yes; a vault or a dome, recognizable at the moment mainly by its shining points. This dome we understand to be the complement or completing part of a correspondent dome on the other side of the world. It follows that we are in the heart of a hollow sphere of loveliest blue, spangled with light. Now the sphere is the one perfect geometrical form. Over and round us then we have the one perfect shape. I do not say it is put there for the purpose of representing God; I say it is there of necessity, because of its nature, and its nature is its relation to God. It is of God's thinking; and that half-sphere above men's heads, with influence endlessly beyond the reach of their consciousness, is the beginning of all revelation of Him to men. They must begin with that. It is the simplest as well as most external likeness of Him, while its relation to Him goes so deep that it represents things in His very nature that nothing else could."

(WM, 213–14)

91. Think then how it would be if this blue sky were plainly a solid. Men of old believed it a succession of hollow spheres, one outside the other; it is hardly a wonder they should have had little gods. No matter how high the value of the inclosing sphere; limited at all it could not declare the glory of God, it could only show His handiwork. In our day it is a sphere only to the eyes; it is a foreshortening of infinitude that it may enter our sight; there is no imagining of a limit to it; it is a sphere only in this, that in no one direction can we come nearer to its circumference than in another. This infinitive sphere, I say then, or, if you like it better, this spheric infinitude, is the only figure, image, emblem, symbol, fit to begin us to know God; it is an idea incomprehensible; we can only believe in it. In like manner God cannot by searching be found out, cannot be grasped by any mind, yet is ever before us, the one we can best know, the one we must know, the one we cannot help knowing; for His end in giving us being is that His humblest creature should at length possess Himself, and be possessed by Him.

(WM, 214)

92. "If it were not for the outside world," resumed Ian, "we should have no inside world to understand things by. Least of all could we understand God without these millions of sights and sounds and scents and motions, weaving their endless harmonies. They come out from His heart to let us know a little of what is in it!"

(WM, 214)

93. The season went on, and the world, like a great flower afloat in space, kept opening its thousandfold blossom. Hail and sleet were things lost in the distance of the year— storming away in some far-off region of the north, unknown

to the summer generation. The butterflies, with wings looking as if all the flower-painters of fairyland had wiped their
brushes upon them in freakful yet artistic sport, came forth
in the freedom of their wills and the faithful ignorance of
their minds. The birds, the poets of the animal creation—
what though they never get beyond the lyrical!—awoke to
utter their own joy, and awake like joy in others of God's
children. The birds grew silent, because their history laid
hold upon them, compelling them to turn their words into
deeds, and keep eggs warm, and hunt for worms. The butterflies died of old age and delight. The green life of the
earth rushed up on corn to be ready for the time of need.
The corn grew ripe, and therefore weary, hung its head,
died, and was laid aside for a life beyond its own. The keen
sharp old morning and nights of autumn came back as they
had come so many thousand times before, and made human limbs strong and human hearts sad and longing.
Winter would soon be near enough to stretch out a long
forefinger once more, and touch with the first frosty shiver
some little child that loved summer, and shrunk from the
cold.

(AF, 141)

94. He was now leading on the blessed season of spring,
when the earth would be almost heaven enough to those
who had passed through the fierceness of the winter. Even
now, the winter, old and weary, was halting away before the
sweet approaches of the spring—a symbol of that eternal
spring before whose slow footsteps Death itself, "the winter
of our discontent," shall vanish.

(AF, 130)

95. It was a sweet fresh morning, late in spring—those
loveliest of hours that unite the seasons, like the shimmer-
ing question of green or blue in the feathers of a
peacock. . . . The sun was but a few degrees above the horizon, shining with all his heart, and the earth was taking the
shine with all hers. "I too, am light," she was saying,

"although I can but receive it." The trees were covered with baby-leaves, half wrapped in their swaddling clothes, and their breath was a warm aromatic odour in the glittering air. The air and the light seemed one, and Malcolm felt as if his soul were breathing the light into its very depths, while his body was drinking in the soft spicy wind. . . . And the song of the larks was one with the light and air. The budding of the trees was their way of singing; but the larks beat them at that. "What a power of joy," thought Malcolm, "there must be in God, to be able to keep so many larks so full of bliss!" . . . Then he said to himself: "The larks do not make their own singing; do mortals make their own sighing?" And he saw that at least they might open wider the doors of their hearts to the Perseus Joy that comes to slay the grief-monsters.

(ML, 162–63)

96. When the gentle, washing wind blew upon Annie, she thought of the wind that bloweth where it listeth; and that, if ever the Spirit of God blew upon her, she would feel it just like that wind of summer sunset—so cool, so blessed, so gentle, so living! And was it not God that breathed that wind upon her? Was He not even then breathing His Spirit into the soul of that woman-child?

(AF, 219)

97. It was perhaps the loveliest of all hours in the year. The summer was young and soft, and this was the warmest evening they had yet had—dusky, dark even below, while above, the stars were bright and large and sharp in the blackest blue sky. The night came close around them, clasping them in one universal arm of love, and although it neither spoke nor smiled, seemed all eye and ear, seemed to see and hear and know everything they said and did. It is a way the night has sometimes, and there is a reason for it.

(PC, 36)

98. The summer at length reigned lordly in the land. The roses were in bloom, from the black purple to the warm white. Ah, the roses! He must indeed be a God who invented the roses. They sank into the red hearts of men and women, caused old men to sigh, young men to long, and women to weep with strange ecstatic sadness....

The winds were soft and odor laden. The wide meadows through which flowed the river, seemed to smite the eye with their greenness; and the black and red and white kine bent down their sleek necks among the marsh-marigolds and the meadow-sweet and the hundred lovely things that border the level water-courses, and fed on the blessed grass.

(PF, 136)

99. The sun was still reveling in the gift of himself. A thin blue mist went up to greet him, like the first of the smoke from the altars of the morning. The fields lay yellow below; the rich colours of decay hung heavy on the woods, and seemed to clothe them as with the trappings of a majestic sorrow; but the spiderwebs sparkled with dew, and the gossamer films floated thick in the level sunbeams....

The sun, like a householder leaving his house for a time, was burning up a thousand outworn things before he went; hence the smoke of the dying hearth of summer was going up to the heavens; but there was a heart of hope left, for, when farthest away, the sun is never gone, and the snow is the earth's blanket against the frost.

(M, 231–32)

100. The day was one of God's odes—written for men. Would that the days of our human autumn were as calmly grand, as gorgeously hopeful as the days that lead the aging year down to the grave of winter! If our white hairs were sunlit from behind like those radiance-bordered clouds; if our air were as pure as this when it must be as cold; if the falling at last of longest-cherished hopes did but, like that of the forest leaves, let in more of the infinite possibilities

of the region of truth which is the matrix of fact; we should go marching down the hill of life like a battered but still bannered army marching on its way home. But alas! how often we rot, instead of march towards the grave!

(M, 231)

101. It was a sunny, frosty morning. The snow had fallen all night with its own silence, and no wind had interfered with the gracious alighting of the feathery water. Every branch, every twig, was laden with its sparkling burden of down-flickered flakes, and threw long lovely shadows on the smooth featureless dazzle below. Away, away, stretched the outspread glory, the only darkness in it being the line of the winding river. All the snow that fell on it vanished, as death and hell shall one day vanish in the fire of God. It flowed on, black through its banks of white. Away again stretched the shine to the town, where every roof had the sheet that was let down from heaven spread over it, and the streets lay a foot deep in yet unsullied snow, soon, like the story of the ages, to be trampled, soiled, wrought, and driven with human feet, till, at last, God's strong sun would wipe it all away.

(AF, 63)

102. (After a difficult period in his life, a minister meditates on his experience.)

He thought afterwards, when the time had passed, that surely in this period of darkness he had been visited and upheld by a power whose presence and even influence escaped his consciousness. He knew not how else he could have got through it. Also he remembered that strange helps had come to him; that the aspects of nature then wonderfully softened towards him, that then first he began to feel sympathy with her ways and shows, and to see in them all the working of a diffused humanity. He remembered how once a hawthorn-bud set him weeping; and how once, as he went miserable to church, a child looked up in his face and

smiled, and how in the strength of that smile he had walked
boldly to the lectern.

(TW, 59)

103. Mingled with all the noises of dogs and horses, came a
soft nestling murmur that filled up the interspaces of sound
which even their tumult could not help leaving. . . . Malcolm
heard it, and it filled all the interspaces of his soul with a
speechless delight. He knew it for the still small voice of the
awful sea.

(ML, 164)

104. It was a day when everything around seemed almost
perfect: everything does, now and then, come nearly right
for a moment or two, preparatory to coming all right for
good at the last. It was the third week in June. The great
furnace was glowing and shining in full force, driving the
ship of our life at her best speed through the ocean of
space. For on deck, and between decks, and aloft, there is
so much going on at one time than at another, that I may
well say she was then going at her best speed, for there is
quality as well as rate in motion. The trees were well
clothed, most of them in their very best. Their garments
were soaking up the light and the heat, and the wind was
going about among them, telling now one and now another,
that all was well, and getting through an immense amount
of comfort-work in a single minute. It said a word or two to
myself as often as it passed me, and made me happier than
any boy I know just at present, for I was an old man, and
ought to be more easily made happy than any mere
beginner.

(RS, 13)

105. Nobody quite knows the beauty of a country, especially a quiet country, except one who has been born in it, or
for whom at least childhood and boyhood and youth have
opened door after door into the hidden phases of its life.
There is no square yard on the face of the earth but

someone can in part understand what God meant in making it; while the same changeful skies canopy the most picturesque and the dullest landscapes; the same winds wake and blow over desert and pasture land, making the bosoms of youth and age swell with the delight of their blowing. The winds are not all so full as are some of delicious odours gathered as they pass from gardens, fields, and hillsides; but all have their burden of sweetness. Those that blew upon little Clare were oftener filled with the smell of farmyards, and burning weeds and cottage-fires, than of flowers; but never would one of such odours revisit him without bringing fresh delight to his heart. . . . He was one of those who, regarding what a thing *is,* and not comparing it with other things, descry the thought of God in it, and love it; for to love what is beautiful is as natural as to love our mothers.

(RS, 57)

106. Whoever loves the truth must love shining things! God is the Father of lights, even of the lights hid in the dark earth—sapphires and rubies, and all the families of splendour.

(WM, 338)

107. It was a lovely day. The sun shone so warm that you could not help thinking of what he would be able to do before long—draw primroses and buttercups out of the earth by force of sweet persuasive influences. But in the shadows lay fine webs and laces of ice, so delicately lovely that one could not but be glad of the cold that made the water able to please itself by taking such graceful forms and I wondered over again for the hundredth time what could be the principle which, in the wildest, most lawless, fantastically chaotic, apparently capricious work of nature, always kept it beautiful. The beauty of holiness must be at the heart of it somehow, I thought. Because our God is so free from stain, so loving, so unselfish, so good, so altogether what He wants us to be, so holy, therefore all His works

declare Him in beauty; His fingers can touch nothing but to
mould it into loveliness; and even the play of His elements
is in grace and tenderness of form.

(AN, 211)

108. ... never, in the midst of the good things of this lovely world, have I felt quite at home in it. Never has it shown
me things lovely or grand enough to satisfy me. It is not all
I should like for a place to live in. It may be that my
unsatisfaction comes from not having eyes open enough, or
keen enough, to see and understand what He has given; but
it matters little whether the cause lie in the world or in
myself, both being incomplete: God is, and all is well.

(SIII, 261)

109. The sorrows are sickly things and die, while the joys
are strong divine children and shall live forever.

(MM, 454)

110. Beauty is one of the surest antidotes to vexation. Often when life looked dreary about me, from some real or
fancied injustice or indignity, has a thought of truth been
flashed into my mind from a flower, a shape of frost, or
even a lingering shadow,—not to mention such glories as
angel-winged clouds, rainbows, stars, and sunrises.

(SG, 437)

111. The western sky was smoky red; the stars were coming out; the wind was mild, and seemed to fill her soul with
life from the fountain of life, from God Himself.

(TB, 598)

112. Was there ever a happier man than Joseph that night
as he strode along the footpath? A day of invigorating and
manly toil behind him, folded up in the sense of work ac-
complished; a clear sky overhead, beginning to breed stars;
the pale amber hope of tomorrow's sunrise low down in the
west; a frosty air around him, challenging to the surface the

glow of the forge which his day's labor had stored in his body; his heart and brain at rest with his Father in heaven; his precious violin under his arm; before him the welcoming parlor, where two sweet women waited his coming, one of them the brightest angel, in or out of heaven, to him; and the prospect of a long evening of torrent-music between them—who I repeat, could have been more blessed, heart, and soul, and body, than Joseph Jasper? His being was an all-sided lens concentrating all joys in the one heart of his consciousness. God only knows how blessed He could make us if we would but let Him!

(MM, 453–54)

113. (A conversation between two Scottish fishermen after four days in London.)

"Eh, my lord!" said Blue Peter.... "It's like a month since I was at the church. I'm afraid the din's gotten into my head, and I'll never get it out again. I could almost wish I was a mackerel, for they tell me the fish hears nothing. I know well now what you meant, my lord, when you said you feared the din might make you forget your Maker."

"I have been wishing myself, these last two days," responded Malcolm, "that I could get one sight of the waves clashing upon the rocks. The din of nature never troubles the good thoughts in you. I reckon it's because it's a kind of harmony in itself, and all harmony's just as the schoolmaster used to say, a higher kind of peace.... But this noise tumultuous of human strife, this din of iron shoes and iron wheels, this whurr and whuzz of buying and selling and getting gain—it doesn't help a body to their prayers.... Aye, but I doubt there's something not right about it, Peter," returned Malcolm.... "I had the whole thing through my head last night and I can't but think there's something wrong with a man if he can't hear the word of God as well in the midst of a multitude ... all made in the image of the Father, as in the heart of wind and water and the heavens and stars and all. You can't say that those things are made in the image of God, in the same way, at least, that you can say it of the body and face of a man, for through them the God of the whole earth revealed Himself in Christ. . . . I remember well how Mr. Graham said to me once that there was something of Him that made Him looking out of each man that He had made. . . ."

"Well I don't know; but anyway I can't think it can be against the truth of the gospel to wish yourself more alone with your God than you can ever be in such an awful Babylon of a place like this."

"No, no, Peter; I'm not saying that. I know well we're to go into the closet and shut the door. I'm only afraid that there is something wrong in myself to take it so ill to be among so many neighbors. I'm thinking that, if all was right within me, if I loved my neighbor as the Lord would have them that loved Him love each his own brother, I might be better able to pray among them—aye, in the very face of the bargaining and lying all about me."

(ML*, 44–45)

---

*Indicates translation of Scottish dialect into English.

THREE

 TRUTH

114. (A fragment of conversation concerning beauty and truth.)

"If I thought the sweetest air on the violin had no truth in it, I could not listen to it a moment longer."

"Of course the air has all the truth it pretends to—the truth, that is, of the relations of sounds and of intervals—also, of course, the truth of its relation as a whole to that creative something in the human mind which gave birth to it."

"That is not all it pretends. It pretends that the something it gives birth to in the human mind is also a true thing."

(PF, 82)

115. [In art] the fundamental idea seems to be the revelation of the true through the beautiful.

(DO, 196)

116. The very essence of poetry is truth, and as soon as a word is not true, it's not poetry, though it may have the clothes of it.

(SG, 359)

117. I believe with all my heart that the true is the beautiful, and that nothing evil can be other than ugly. If it seems not so, it is in virtue of some good mingled with the evil, and not in the smallest degree in virtue of the evil.

(AN, 155)

118. As beauty and truth are one, so are truth and strength one.

(DG, 137)

119. If it be the truth, we shall one day see it another thing than it appears now, and love it because we see it lovely; for *all* truth is lovely.

(SI, 70)

120. (The narrator describes some music heard in fairyland and then makes the following comments.)

As in all sweetest music, a tinge of sadness was in every note. Nor do we know how much of the pleasures even of life we owe to the intermingled sorrows. Joy cannot unfold the deepest truths, although deepest truth must be deepest joy.

(PH, 67)

121. There must be things so entirely beyond our capacity, that we cannot now see enough of them to be able even to say that they are incomprehensible. There must be millions of truths that have not yet risen above the horizon of what we call the finite.

(TB, 316)

122. Our vision is so circumscribed, our theories are so small—the garment of them not large enough to wrap us in; our faith so continually fashions itself to the fit of our dwarf intellect, that there is endless room for rebellion against ourselves: we must not let our poor knowledge limit our not so poor intellect, our intellect limit our faith, our faith

limit our divine hope; reason must humbly watch over all—reason, the candle of the Lord.

(SII, 90)

123. . . . repose is not the end of education; its end is a noble unrest, an ever renewed awaking from the dead a ceaseless questioning of the past for the interpretation of the future. . . .

(DO, 1)

124. I cannot admit for a moment that there is anything in the Bible too mysterious to be looked into; for the Bible is a *revelation,* an unveiling. True, into many things uttered there I can see only a little way. But that little way is the way of life; for the depth of their mystery is God.

(SI, 72)

125. There is more hid in Christ than we shall ever learn, here or there either; but they that begin first to inquire will soonest be gladdened with revelation; and with them He will be best pleased, for the slowness of His disciples troubled Him of old. To say that we must wait for the other world, to know the mind of Him who came to this world to give Himself to us, seems to me that foolishness of a worldly and lazy spirit. The Son of God *is* the Teacher of men, giving to them of His Spirit—that Spirit which manifests the deep things of God. . . .

(SI, 54)

126. Our Lord had no design of constructing a system of truth in intellectual forms. . . . He spoke out of a region of realities which He knew could only be suggested—not represented—in the forms of intellect and speech. With vivid flashes of life and truth His words invade our darkness, rousing us with sharp stings of light to will our awaking, to arise from the dead and cry for the light which He can give,

not in the lightning of words only, but in indwelling presence and power.

(SI, 66–67)

127. You know what Christ requires of you is right—much
of it at least you believe to be right, and your duty to do,
whether He said it or not: *do it.* If you do not do what you
know of the truth, I do not wonder that you seek it intellectually, for that kind of search may well be, as Milton represents it, a solace even to the fallen angels. But do not call
anything that may be so gained, *the Truth.*

(SIII, 152)

128. If we are bound to search after what our Lord
means—and He speaks that we may understand—we are at
least equally bound to refuse any interpretation which
seems to us unlike Him, unworthy of Him.... Some
misapprehension ... or some slavish adherence to old prej-
udices, may thus cause us to refuse the true interpretation,
but we are none the less bound to refuse and wait for more
light. To accept that as the will of our Lord which to us is
inconsistent with what we have learned to worship in Him
already, is to introduce discord into that harmony whose
end is to unite our hearts, and make them whole.

(SI, 68–69)

129. Obedient to Polwarth's instructions, Wingfold had tak-
en to his New Testament. At first, as he read and sought to
understand, ever and anon some small difficulty, notably,
foremost of all, the discrepancy in the genealogies—I mention it merely to show the sort of difficulty I mean—would
insect-like shoot out of the darkness and sting him in the
face. Some of these he pursued, encountered, crushed—and
found he had gained next to nothing by the victory; and
Polwarth soon persuaded him to let such alone for the
present, seeing they involved nothing concerning the Man
at a knowledge of whom it was his business to arrive. But
when it came to the perplexity caused by some of the

sayings of Jesus Himself, it was another matter. He *must* understand the Man. Here Polwarth told him that possibly the meaning of the words was beyond him, and that the understanding of them depended on a more advanced knowledge of Jesus Himself. . . . Between the mind and the understanding of certain hard utterances, therefore, there must of necessity lie a gradation of easier steps.

(TW, 145)

130. The man who is anxious to hold every point, will speedily bring a question to a mere dispute about trifles, leaving the real matter, whose elements may appeal to the godlike in every man, out in the cold. Such a man, having gained his paltry point, will crow like the bantam he is, while the other, who may be the greater, perhaps the better man, although in the wrong, is embittered by his smallness, and turns away with increased prejudice. Human nature can hardly be blamed for its readiness to impute to the case the shallowness of its pleader. Few men do more harm than those who, taking the right side, dispute for personal victory, and argue, as they are sure then to do, ungenerously. But even genuine unbelief is thus assailed, likely to be brought thereby into any mood, but one unfit for receiving it. God alone can convince, and till the full time is come for the birth of the truth in a soul, the words of even the Lord Himself are not there potent.

(PF, 156)

131. The recognition of a living Master is far more than any notions about Him. In the worship of Him a thousand truths are working, unknown and yet active, which embodied in theory, and dissociated from the living mind that was in Christ, will as certainly breed worms as any omer of hoarded manna.

(EA, 6)

132. Fact at best is but a garment of truth, which has ten thousand changes of raiment woven in the same loom. Let

the dreamer only do the truth of his dream, and one day he will realize all that is worth realizing in it—and a great deal more and better than it contained.

(WM, 29)

133. To inquire into what God has made is the main function of the imagination. It is aroused by facts, is nourished by facts, seeks for higher and yet higher laws in those facts; but refuses to regard science as the sole interpreter of nature, or the laws of science as the only region of discovery.

(DO, 2)

134. The man who will not speculate at all, can make no progress. The thinking about the possible is as genuine as lawful, and perhaps as edifying an exercise of the mind as the severest induction. . . . Experiment itself must follow in the track of sober conjecture; for if we know already, where is the good of experiment?

(MOL, 159–60)

135. To him a man's imagination was of no higher calling than to amuse him with its vagaries. He did not know, apparently, that Imagination had been the guide to all the physical discoveries which he worshipped, therefore could not reason that perhaps she might be able to carry a glimmering light into the forest of the supersensible.

(TW, 32)

136. But now that Conscience had got up into the guard's seat, and Will had taken the reins, he found all his intellectual faculties in full play, keeping well together, leads up and traces tight, while the outrider, Imagination, with his spotted dog Fancy, was always far ahead, but never beyond the sound of the guard's horn; and ever as they went, object after object hitherto beyond the radius of his interest rose

on the horizon of question, and began to glimmer in the dawn of human relation.

(TW, 178)

137. For what else is our imagination given us but the discovery of good reasons that are, or the invention of good reasons that may perhaps be!

(TW, 485)

138. It is God who gives thee thy mirror of imagination, and if thou keep it clean, it will give thee back no shadow but of the truth.

(PF, 29)

139. We had spoken a good deal together about the infancy and childhood of Jesus, about the shepherds, and the wise men, and the star in the east, and the children of Bethlehem. I encouraged the thoughts of all the children to rest and brood upon the fragments that are given us, and, believing that the imagination is one of the most powerful of all the faculties for aiding the growth of the truth in the mind, I would ask them questions as to what they thought He might have said or done in ordinary family occurrences, thus giving a reality in their minds to this part of His history, and trying to rouse in them a habit of referring their conduct to the standard of His. If we do not thus employ our imagination on sacred things, His example can be of no use to us except in exactly corresponding circumstances— and when can such occur from one end to another of our lives? The very effort to think how He would have done, is a wonderful purifier of conscience, and, even if the conclusion arrived at should not be correct from lack of sufficient knowledge of His character and principles, it will be better than any that can be arrived at without this inquiry.

(SP, 70–71)

140. (A spiritually mature man is asked if he can imagine any good reason why we are kept in ignorance about what life after death is like.)

"I think I know one," answered Polwarth. "I have sometimes fancied it might be because no true idea of their condition could possibly be grasped by those who remain in the tabernacle of the body; that to know their state it is necessary that we should also be clothed in our new bodies. . . . I doubt if we have any words in which the new facts could be imparted to our knowledge, the facts themselves being beyond the reach of any senses whereof we are now in possession. I expect to find my new body provided with new, I mean *other* senses beyond which I now possess; many more may be required to bring us into relation with all the facts in Himself which God may have shadowed forth in properties, as we say, of what we call matter? The spaces all around us, even those betwixt star and star, may be the home of the multitudes of the heavenly host, yet seemingly empty to all who have but our provision of senses."

(TW, 485–86)

141. I doubt much if mere opposition to the false is of any benefit. Convince a man by argument that the thing he has been taught is false, and you leave his house empty, swept, and garnished; but the expulsion of the falsehood is no protection against its re-entrance in another mask, with seven worse than itself in its company. The right effort of the teacher is to give the positive—to present, as he may, the vision of reality, for the perception of which, and not for the discovery of falsehood, is man created. This will not only cast out the demon, but so people the house that he will not dare return. . . . It is the positive by which a man shall live. Truth is his life.

(EA, 171)

142. Whatever good may lie in the destroying of the false, the best hammer of the iconoclast will not serve withal to

carve the celestial form of the Real; and when the iconoclast becomes the bigot of negation, and declares the non-
existence of any form worthy of worship, because he has
destroyed so many unworthy, he passes into a fool. That he
has never conceived a deity such as he could worship, is a
poor ground to any but the man himself for saying such
cannot exist; and to him it is but a ground lightly vaulted
over the vacuity of self-importance. Such a divine form may
yet stand in the adytum of this or that man whom he and
the world count an idiot.

(TB, 225)

143. There is this difference between the growth of some
human beings and that of others: in the one case it is a
continuous dying, in the other a continuous resurrection.
One of the latter sort comes at length to know at once
whether a thing is true the moment it comes before him;
one of the former class grows more and more afraid of
being taken in, so afraid of it that he takes himself in altogether, and comes at length to believe in nothing but his
dinner: to be sure of a thing with him is to have it between
his teeth.

(PC, 19–20)

144. He cared for nothing but the truth, and yet he could
never assure himself that anything was true. The more likely a thing looked to be true, the more anxious was he that it
should be unassailable; and his fertile mind would in as
many moments throw a score of objections at it, looking
after each with eager eyes as if pleading for a refutation. It
was the very love of what was good that generated in him
doubt and anxiety.

(WC, 161)

145. "Perhaps some people can see things other people
can't see. . . ."

(PG, 158)

146. "We are all very anxious to be understood, and it is very hard not to be. But there is one thing much more necessary."

"What is that, grandmother?"

"To understand other people."

(PG, 151)

147. There are many true things that cannot be seen with the naked eye! The eye must be clothed and in its right mind first!

(HA, 280)

148. A man must be good to see truth.

(EA, 242)

149. His eye is fixed on the truth. . . . While a man looks thitherward, all the movements of his spirit reveal themselves only in peace.

(EA, 194)

150. . . . to him who has once seen even a shadow only of the truth, and, even but hoping he has seen it when it is present no longer, tries to obey it—to him the real vision, the Truth Himself, will come, and depart no more, but abide with him for ever.

(L, 235)

151. Shall a man climb the last flight of the stair who has never set foot on the lowest step? Truth is one, and he who does the truth in the small thing is of the truth; he who will do it only in a great thing, who postpones the small thing near him to the great thing farther from him, is not of the truth.

(SII, 53)

152. We need not trouble ourselves about our hearts, and all their varying hues and shades of feeling. Truth is at the root of all existence, therefore everything must come right

if only we are obedient to the truth; and right is the deepest satisfaction of every creature as well as of God. I wait in confidence. If things be not as we think, they will both arouse and satisfy a better *think,* making us glad they are not as we expected.

(FS, 32)

153. The moment she laid hold of a truth—the moment, that is, when it was no longer another's idea, but her own perception—it began to sprout in her in all directions of practice. By nature she was not intellectually quick; but, because such was her character, the ratio of her progress was of necessity an increasing one.

(MM, 46)

154. He rose in the morning with the feeling revived, that something intense was going on all around. But the door into life generally opens behind us, and a hand is put forth which draws us in backwards. The sole wisdom for man or boy who is haunted with the hovering of unseen wings, with the scent of unseen roses, and the subtle enticements of "melodies unheard," is *work.* If he follow any of those, they will vanish. But if he work, they will come unsought, and, while they come, he will believe that there is a fairy-land, where poets find their dreams, and prophets are laid hold of by their visions. The idle beat their heads against its walls, or mistake the entrance, and go down into the dark places of the earth . . . to no mere onlooker will Life any more than fairy-land open its secret. A man must become an actor before he can be a true spectator.

(AF, 148)

155. "You try to work upon people's feelings without reference to their judgment. Anyone who can preach what you call rousing sermons, is considered a grand preacher amongst you, and there is a great danger of his being led thereby to talk more nonsense than sense. And when the excitement goes off, there is no seed left in the soil to grow

in peace, and they are always craving after more excitement."

"Well, there is the preacher to rouse them up again."

"And the consequence is, that they continued like children—the good ones, I mean—and have hardly a chance of making a calm, deliberate choice of that which is good; while those who have been only excited and nothing more, are hardened and seared by the recurrence of such feeling as is neither aroused by truth nor followed by action."

(SP, 307)

156. Religion is no way of life, no show of life, no observance of any sort. It is neither the food nor the medicine of being. It is life essential. To think otherwise is as if a man should pride himself on his honesty, or his parental kindness, or hold up his head amongst men because he never killed one: were he less than honest or kind or free from blood, he would yet think something of himself! The man to whom virtue is but the ornament of character, something over and above, not essential to it, is not yet a man.

(ML, 311)

157. The honesty in which a man can pride himself must be a small one, for more honesty will ever reveal more defect, while perfect honesty will never think of itself at all.

(ML, 323)

158. "The truth's the truth," resumed Miss Horn, "neither more nor less."

"Aye," responded Malcolm, "but there's a right and a wrong time for the telling of it."

(ML*, 10)

159. I was not at all sure that a lie in defense of the innocent, and to prevent the knowledge of what no one has any right to know, was wrong—seeing such involves no injus-

_____

*Indicates translation of Scottish dialect into English.

tice on the one side and does justice on the other. I have seen reason since to change my mind, and count my liberty restricted to silence. . . . I now think that to lie is, as it were, to snatch the reins out of God's hand.

(WC, 347)

160. We are not bound to say all we think, but we are bound not even to look what we do not think.

(SIII, 107–8)

161. I did not show all my dissatisfaction, however, for that would only have estranged us; and it is not required, nay it may be wrong, to show all you feel or think: what is required of us is, not to show what we do not feel or think; for that is to be false.

(AN, 240)

162. I would not favor a fiction to keep a world out of hell. The hell that a lie would keep any man out of is doubtless the very best place for him to go. It is the truth, yes The Truth that saves the world.

(AN, 144)

163. Is every Christian expected to bear witness? A man content to bear no witness to the truth is not in the kingdom of heaven. One who believes must bear witness.

(SIII, 107)

164. The true king is the man who stands up a true man and speaks the truth, and will die but not lie.

(SIII, 105)

165. Half the misery in the world comes from trying to look, instead of trying to be, what one is not.

(FS, 1)

166. Often without knowing it, (some people) judge life, and truth itself by the falsest of measures, namely the judg-

ment of others falser than themselves; they do not ask what is true or right, but what folk think and say about this or that. James, for instance, altogether missed being a gentleman by his habit of asking himself how, in such circumstances, a gentleman would behave. As the man of honor he would fain know himself to be, he would never tell a lie or break a promise; but he had not come to perceive that there are other things as binding as a promise.... He did not, for instance, mind raising expectations which he had not the least intention of fulfilling.

(SF, 19)

167. What is hypocrisy? The desire to look better than you are; the hiding of things you do, because you would not be supposed to do them, because you would be ashamed to have them known where you are known. The doing of them is foul; the hiding of them, in order to appear better than you are, is fouler still.

(SIII, 231)

168. For a man to *grow* a gentleman, it is of great consequence that his grandfather should have been an honest man; but if a man *be* a gentleman, it matters little what his grandfather or grandmother either was. Nay—if a man be a gentleman, it is of the smallest consequence, except for its own sake, whether the world counts him one or not.

(WM, 7)

169. Are we careful to be true? Do we endeavour to live to the height of our ideas? Or are we mean, self-serving, world-flattering, fawning slaves?

(SIII, 107)

170. Do you so love the truth and the right, that you welcome, or at least submit willingly to the idea of an exposure of what in you is yet unknown to yourself—an exposure that may redound to the glory of the truth by making you ashamed and humble?

(SIII, 235–36)

171. (The following shows how difficult it is for a wicked person to know the truth about himself.)

A man may sink by such slow degrees that, long after he is a devil, he may go on being a good church-man ... and thinking himself a good Christian.

(SIII, 242)

172. Let us be true, whatever come of it, and look the facts of things in the face! If I am a poor creature, let me be content to know it! For have I not the joy that God can make me great! And is not the first step toward greatness, to refuse to call that great which is not great? ... Let us confess ourselves that which we cannot consent to remain! The confession of not being, is the sole foundation for becoming. Self is a quicksand; God is the only rock.

(HA, 242)

FOUR

 FAITH

173. (In a fairy tale, we find a grand image of faith.)

Then the Old Man of the Earth stopped over the floor of the cave, raised a huge stone from it, and left it leaning. It disclosed a great hole that went plumb-down.

"That is the way," he said.

"But there are no stairs."

"You must throw yourself in. There is no other way."

She turned and looked him full in the face—stood so for a whole minute, as she thought: it was a whole year—then threw herself head-long into the hole.

(GK, 36–37)

174. That man is perfect in faith who can come to God in the utter death of his feelings and his desires, without a glow or an aspiration, with the weight of low thoughts,

failures, neglects, and wandering forgetfulness, and say to Him, "Thou art my refuge, because Thou art my home."

(SI, 25)

175. ... to hold a thing with the intellect, is not to believe it. A man's real belief is that which he lives by....

(SII, 239)

176. To believe in Him is to do as He does, to follow Him where He goes. We must believe in Him *practically*—altogether practically, as He believed in His Father; not as one concerning whom we have to hold something, but as one whom we have to follow out of the body of this death into life eternal. It is not to follow Him to take Him in any way theoretically, to hold this or that theory about why He died, or wherein lay His atonement: such things can be revealed only to those who follow Him in His active being and the principles of His life—who do as He did, live as He lived. There is no other following.

(SII, 218–19)

177. When I was a younger man I used to go out with the fishing boats now and then, drawn chiefly by my love for the boy, who earned his bread that way before he was in his teens. One night we were caught in a terrible storm, and had to stand out to sea in the pitch dark. He was then not fourteen. "Can you let a boy like that steer?" I said to the captain of the boat. "Yes; just a boy like that," he answered. "Malcolm will steer as straight as an arrow." When he was relieved, he crept over to where I sat. "Is there any true definition of a straight line, sir?" he said. "I can't take the one in my Euclid."—"So you're not afraid, Malcolm?" I returned, heedless of his question, for I wanted to see what he would answer. "Afraid, sir!" he rejoined with some surprise, "I would not like to hear the Lord say, *O thou of little faith!*"—"But," I persisted, "God may mean to drown you!"—"And why should I not? If you were to tell me that I

might be drowned without his meaning it, I would be frightened enough."

(ML*, 253–54)

178. (MacDonald holds a conversation with his reader.)

The care that is filling your mind at this moment, or but waiting till you lay the book aside to leap upon you—that need which is no need, is a demon sucking at the spring of your life.

"No; mine is a reasonable care—an unavoidable care, indeed!"

"Is it something you have to do this very moment?"

"No."

"Then you are allowing it to usurp the place of something that is required of you this moment!"

"There is nothing required of me at this moment."

"Nay, but there is—the greatest thing that can be required of man."

"Pray, what is it?"

"Trust in the living God. His will is your life."

"He may not will I should have what I need!"

"Then you only think you need it. Is it a good thing?"

"Yes, it is a good thing."

"Then why doubt you shall have it?"

"Because God may choose to have me go without it."

"Why should He?"

"I cannot tell."

"Must it not be in order to give you something instead?"

"I want nothing instead."

"I thought I was talking to a Christian!"

"I can consent to be called nothing else."

"Do you not, then, know that, when God denies anything a child of His values, it is to give him something *He* values?"

"But if I do not want it? . . ."

---

*Indicates translation of Scottish dialect into English.

"If thou art not willing that God should have His way with thee, then, in the name of God, be miserable—till thy misery drive thee to the arms of the Father."

(SII, 49–51)

179. (In the following segment of a conversation, a curate is speaking to an unbeliever.)

If there be a God, truth must be joy. If there be not, truth may be misery.—But, honestly, I know not one advanced Christian who tries to obey for the hope of Heaven or the fear of hell. Such ideas have long vanished from such a man. He loves God; he loves truth; he loves his fellow, and knows he must love him more. You judge of Christianity either by those who are not true representatives of it and are indeed, less of Christians than yourself; or by others who, being intellectually inferior . . . belie Christ with their dull theories concerning Him. Yet the latter may have in them a noble seed, urging them up heights to you at present unconceived and inconceivable; while, in the meantime, some of them serve their generation well, and do as much for those that are to come after as you do yourself.

(PF, 210)

180. (Following are comments on the fact that the New Testament records no information about the after-death experiences of those who were raised from the dead.)

When I think of the pictures of heaven drawn from the attempt of prophecy to utter its visions in the poor forms of the glory of earth, I see it better that we should walk by faith, and not by a fancied sight. I judge that the region beyond is so different from ours, so comprising in one surpassing excellence all the goods of ours, that any attempt of the had-been-dead to describe it, would have resulted in the most wretched of misconceptions.

(MOL, 194–95)

181. Doubts are the messengers of the Living One to rouse the honest. They are the first knock at our door of things

that are not yet, but have to be, understood. . . . Doubt must precede every deeper assurance; for uncertainties are what we first see when we look into a region hitherto unknown, unexplored, unannexed.

(SII, 201)

182. (A dying man wishes that he could help Wingfold, a curate who has doubts.)

"Are you any surer about Him, sir, than you used to be?"

"At least I hope in Him far more," answered Wingfold.

"Is that enough?"

"No, I want more."

"I wish I could come back and tell you that I am alive and all is true."

"I would rather have the natural way of it, and get the good of not knowing first."

"But if I could tell you I had found God, then would that make you sure. . . ."

"I think I shall find all I want in Jesus Christ," he said.

"But you can't see Him, you know."

"Perhaps I can do better. And at all events I can wait," said the curate. "Even if He would let me, I would not see Him one moment before He thought best. I would not be out of a doubt or difficulty an hour sooner than He would take me."

(TW, 429–30)

183. Do you long for the assurance of some sensible sign? Do you ask why no intellectual proof is to be had? I tell you that such would but delay, perhaps altogether impair for you, that better, that best, that only vision, into which at last your world must blossom—such a contact, namely, with the heart of God Himself, such a perception of His being, and His absolute oneness with you, the child of His thought, the individuality softly parted from His spirit, yet living still and only by His presence and love, as, by its own radiance, will sweep doubt away forever.

Being then in the light and knowing it, the lack of intellectual proof concerning that which is too high for it, will trouble you no more than would your inability to silence a metaphysician who declared that you had no real existence. It is for the sake of such vision as God would give that you are denied such vision as you would have.

(PF, 231)

184. (The following conversation fragment is between two ladies, one who claims to believe in God but pays no attention to Him, and one who doubts but desires to know.)

"For my part, I would give all I have to know there was a God worth believing in."

"Clementina!"

"What?"

"Of course there is a God. It is very horrible to deny it."

"Which is worse—to deny *it* or to deny *Him?* Now I confess to doubting *it*—that is, the fact of a God; but you seem to me to deny God Himself, for you admit there is a God—think it very wicked to deny that, and yet you don't take interest enough in Him to wish to learn anything about Him. You won't *think*, Florimel. I don't fancy you ever really *think.*"

(ML, 241)

185. ... he was getting rather stupid—one of the chief signs of which was that he believed less and less in things he had never seen.

(PC, 19)

186. Paul Faber was a man who had espoused the cause of science with all the energy of a suppressed poetic nature. He had such a horror of all kinds of intellectual deception or mistake, that he would rather run the risk of rejecting any number of truths than of accepting one error. In this spirit he had concluded that, as no immediate communication had ever reached his eye, or ear, or hand from any

creator of men, he had no ground for believing in the existence of such a creator; while a thousand unfitnesses evident in the world, rendered the existence of one perfectly wise and good and powerful, absolutely impossible. If one said to him that he believed thousands of things he had never himself known, he answered he did so upon testimony. If one rejoined that here too we have testimony, he replied it was not credible testimony, but founded on such experiences as he was justified in considering imaginary, seeing they were like none he had ever had himself. When he was asked whether, while he yet believed there was such a Being as his mother told him of, he had ever set himself to act on that belief, he asserted himself fortunate in the omission of what might have riveted on him the fetters of a degrading faith. For years he had turned his face toward all speculation favoring the non-existence of a creating will, his back toward all tending to show that such a one might be. Argument on the latter side he set down as born of prejudice, and appealing to weakness; on the other as springing from courage, and appealing to honesty. He had never put it to himself which would be the worst deception—to believe there was a God when there was none; or to believe there was no God when there was one.

Thomas Wingfold, the curate, had a great respect for him. Having himself passed through many phases of serious, and therefore painful doubt, he was not as much shocked by the surgeon's unbelief as some whose real faith was even less than Faber's; but he seldom laid himself out to answer his objections. He sought rather, but as yet apparently in vain, to cause the roots of those very objections to stride into, and thus disclose to the man himself, the deeper strata of his being. This might at first only render him the more earnest in his denials, but at length it would probably rouse in him that spiritual nature to which alone such questions belong, and which alone is capable of coping with them.

(PF, 5–6)

187. "What if you should discover . . . that your unbelief has been only indifference and irreverence—and that to a Being grander and nobler and fairer than human heart can conceive?"

"If it be so, let Him punish me," said the doctor gravely.

"If it be so, He will," said the curate solemnly, "—and you will thank Him for it—after a while. The God of my belief is too good not to make Himself known to a man who loves what is fair and honest, as you do."

(PF, 110–11)

188. But I am speaking of those who would fain believe if they could. I ask you, have you been trying the things not seen? Have you been proving them? This is what God put in your hands. He says: "I tell you I am: act you upon that; for I know your conscience moves you to it; act you upon that, and you will find whether I am or not, and what I am."

(GW, 116–17)

189. The very first step towards action is the death-warrant of doubt.

(ML, 24)

190. Do you ask, "What is faith in Him?" I answer, the leaving of your way, your objects, your self, and the taking of His and Him; the leaving of your trust in men, in money, in opinion, in character, in atonement itself, *and doing as He tells you.* I can find no words strong enough to serve for the weight of this necessity—this obedience. It is the one terrible heresy of the church, that it has always been presenting something else than obedience as faith in Christ.

(SII, 243)

191. Faith in its true sense does not belong to the intellect alone, nor to the intellect first, but to the conscience, to the will; and that man is a faithful man who says, "I cannot prove that there is a God, but, O God, if Thou hearest me

anywhere, help me to do Thy will." There is faith. "Do this," and he does it. It is obedience, friends, that is faith; it is doing that thing which you, let me say, even only suppose to be the will of God; for if you are wrong, and do it because you think it is His will, He will set you right. It is the turning of the eye to the light; it is the sending of the feet into the path that is required, putting the hands to do the things which the conscience says ought to be done.

(GW, 117)

192. A man may accept no end of things as facts which are not facts, and his mistakes will not hurt him. He may be unable to receive many facts as facts and neither they nor his refusal of them will hurt him. He may be unable to receive this or that embodiment or form of truth, not having yet grown to its level; but it is no matter so long as when he sees a truth he does it: to see and not do would at once place him in eternal danger. . . . There is in the man who does the truth the radiance of life essential, eternal—a glory infinitely beyond any that can belong to the intellect, beyond any that can even come within its scope to be judged, proven, or denied by it. Through experiences doubtful even to the soul in which they pass, the life may yet be flowing in. To know God is to be in the secret place of all knowledge; and to trust Him changes the atmosphere surrounding mystery and seeming contradiction from one of pain and fear to one of hope: the unknown may be some lovely truth in store for us, which yet we are not good enough to apprehend.

(PF, 361–62)

193. Trust in God. Obey the word—every word of the Master. That is faith; and so believing your opinion will grow out of your true life, and be worthy of it. Peter says the Lord gives the spirit to them that obey Him: the spirit of the Master, and that alone, can guide you to any theory that it will be of use to you to hold.

(SIII, 151)

194. [Abraham's faith] ... was no mere intellectual recognition of the existence of a God ... it was that faith which is one with action: "He went out, not knowing whither he went." The very act of believing in God after such fashion that, when the time of action comes, the man will obey God, is the highest act, the deepest, loftiest righteousness, and the spirit of it will work till the man is perfect.

(SIII, 214)

195. Therefore, friends, the practical thing is just this, and it is the one lesson we have to learn, that, whatever our doubts or difficulties may be, we must do the thing we know in order to learn the thing we do not know. But whether we learn it or not, "If ye know these things," saith the Master, "happy are ye if ye do them." It is the doing that is everything, and the doing is faith, and there is no division between them.

(GW, 117–18)

196. Peace is for those who *do* the truth not those who opine it. The true man troubled by intellectual doubt, is so troubled unto further health and growth. Let him be alive and hopeful, above all obedient, and he will be able to wait for the deeper content which must follow with completer insight.

(PF, 264)

197. If you could prove that there is a God, that implies that you could go all around Him, and buttress up His being with your human argument that He should exist. As soon might a child on his mother's bosom, looking up into his mother's face, write a treatise on what a woman was, and what a mother was.

(GW, 116)

198. (Dorothy, a young woman troubled by doubt, has just begun to help another person who is in the midst of intense suffering.)

The labor of love is its own reward, but Dorothy received much more. For in the fresh impulse and freedom born of this service, she soon found, not only that she thought better and more clearly on the points that troubled her, but that, thus spending herself, she grew more able to believe there must be One whose glory is perfect ministration.... She was not finding an atom of what is called proof; but when the longing heart finds itself able to hope that the perfect is the fact, that the truth is alive, that the lovely is rooted in eternal purpose, it can go on without such proof as belongs to a lower stratum of things, and can not be found in these. When we rise into the mountain air, we require no other testimony than that of our lungs that we are in a healthful atmosphere. We do not find it necessary to submit it to a quantitative analysis; we are content that we breathe with joy, that we grow in strength, become lighter-hearted and better-tempered. Truth is a very different thing from fact; it is the loving contact of the soul independently of all faculty or qualification there for setting it forth or defending it. Truth in the inward parts is a power not an opinion....

(PF, 264)

199. (The following contains a description of Dorothy's spiritual condition after a period of doubt in her life.)
Some of [her difficulties] ... she could hardly recall.... She had been lifted into a region above that wherein moved the questions which had then disturbed her peace. From a point of clear vision, she saw the things themselves so different, that those questions were no longer relevant. The things themselves misconceived, naturally no satisfaction can be got from meditation upon them, or from answers sought to the questions they suggest. If it be objected that she had no better ground for believing than before, I answer that, if a man should be drawing life from the heart of God, it could matter little though he were unable to give a satisfactory account of the mode of its derivation. That the man lives is enough. That another

denies the existence of any such life save in the man's self-fooled imagination, is nothing to the man that lives it. His business is not to raise the dead, but to live—not to convince the blind that there is such a faculty as sight, but to make good use of his eyes. He may not have an answer to any one objection raised by the adopted children of Science—their adopted mother raised none ... but there is no more need that that should trouble him, than that a child should doubt his bliss at his mother's breast, because he can not give the chemical composition of the milk he draws: that in the thing which is the root of his bliss is rather beyond chemistry. ... If there be truth, that truth must ... exercise its own blessing upon the soul which receives it in loyal understanding—that is, in obedience.

(PF, 359–60)

200. The Father of our spirits is not content that we should know Him as we know each other. There is a better, closer, nearer than any human way of knowing, and to that He is guiding us across all the swamps of our unteachableness, the seas of our faithlessness, the desert of our ignorance. Is it so very hard that we should have to wait for that which we can not yet receive? Shall we complain of the shadows cast upon our souls by the hand and the napkin polishing their mirrors to the receiving of the more excellent glory! Have patience, children of the Father. Pray always and do not faint. The mists and the storms and the cold will pass— the sun and the sky are forever more.

(PF, 232)

201. (A conversation between a doctor, who is an atheist, and a young curate whose faith is weak but growing.)

"Well, all I have to say is, I can't for the life of me see what you want to believe in a God for! It seems to me the world would go on rather better without any such fancy. Look here, now: there is young Spenser—out there at Horwood—a patient of mine. His wife died yesterday—one of the loveliest young creatures you ever saw. The poor fellow is as bad about it as fellow can be. Well, he's one of your sort, and said to me the other day, just as you would have him, 'It's the will of God,' he said, 'and we must hold our peace.' 'Don't talk to me about God,' I said, for I couldn't stand it. 'Do you mean to tell me that if there was a God, He would have taken such a lovely creature as that away from her husband and her helpless infant at the age of two and twenty? I scorn to believe it.' "

"What did he say to that?"

"He turned as white as death, and said never a word."

"Ah! you forgot that you were taking from him his only hope of seeing her again!"

"I certainly did not think of that," said Faber. . . . "My argument to poor Spenser remains—however unwise or indeed cruel it may have been."

"I grant it a certain amount of force—as much exactly as had gone to satisfy the children whom I heard the other day agreeing that Dr. Faber was a very cruel man, for he pulled out nurse's tooth, and gave poor little baby such a nasty, nasty powder!"

"Is that a fair parallel? I must look at it."

"I think it is. What you do is often unpleasant, sometimes most painful, but it does not follow that you are a cruel man, and a hurter instead of a healer of men."

"I think there a fault in the analogy," said Faber. "For here am I nothing but a slave to laws already existing, and compelled to work according to them. It is not my fault, therefore, that the remedies I have to use are unpleasant. But if there be a God, He has the matter in His own hands."

"There is weight and justice in your argument, which may well make the analogy appear at first sight false. But is there no theory possible that should make it perfect?"

"I do not see how there should be any. For, if you say that God is under any such compulsion as I am under, then surely the house is divided against itself, and God is not God any more."

"For my part," said the curate, "I think I *could* believe in a God who did but His imperfect best: in one all power, and not all goodness, I could not believe. But suppose that the design of God involved the perfecting of men as the *children of God—'I said ye are gods'*—that He would have them partakers of His own blessedness in kind—be as to Himself;—suppose His grand idea could not be contented with creatures perfect *only* by His gift, so far as that should reach, and having no willing causal share in the perfection—that is, partaking not at all of God's individuality and free-will and choice of good;—then suppose that suffering were the only way through which the individual soul could be set, in separate and self-individuality, so far apart from God that it might *Will,* and so become a partaker of His singleness and freedom; and suppose that this suffering must be and had been initiated by God's taking His share, and that the infinitely greater share; suppose, next, that God saw the germ of a pure affection, say in your friend and his wife, but saw also that it was a germ so imperfect and weak that it could not encounter the coming frosts and winds of the world without loss and decay, while, if they were parted now for a few years, it would grow and strengthen and expand to the certainty of an infinitely higher and deeper and keener love through the endless ages to follow—so that by suffering should come, in place of contented decline, abortion, and death, a troubled birth of joyous result in health and immortality;—suppose all this, and what then?"

Faber was silent a moment, and then answered, "Your theory has but one fault: it is too good to be true."

"My theory leaves plenty of difficulty, but has no such fault as that. Why, what sort of a God would content you, Mr. Faber? The one idea is too bad, the other too good, to be true. Must you expand and pare until you get one exactly to the measure of yourself ere you can accept it as thinkable or possible? Why, a less God than that would not rest your soul a week. The only possibility of believing in a God seems to me to lie in finding an idea of a God large enough, grand enough, lovely enough to be fit to believe in."

"And have you found such, may I ask?"
"I think I am finding such."
"Where?"
"In the Man of the New Testament."

(TW, 366–69)

FIVE

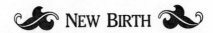 NEW BIRTH

202. We are not and cannot become true sons without our will willing His will, our doing following His making.

(SIII, 13)

203. And we can be sons and daughters . . . only by choosing God for the Father He is, and doing His will—yielding ourselves true sons to the absolute Father. Therein lies human bliss—only and essential. The working out of this our salvation must be pain, and the handing of it down to them that are below must ever be in pain; but the eternal form of the will of God in and for us, is intensity of bliss.

(SIII, 13–14)

204. The Lord Jesus, by free, potent communion with their inmost being, will change His obedient brethren till in every thought and impulse they are good like Him, unselfish, neighbourly, brotherly like Him, loving the Father perfectly like Him, ready to die for the truth like Him, caring like Him for nothing in the universe but the will of God, which is love, harmony, liberty, beauty, and joy.

(SIII, 55)

205. The notion that the salvation of Jesus is a salvation from the consequences of our sins, is a false, mean, low notion. The salvation of Christ is salvation from the smallest tendency or leaning to sin. It is a deliverance into the pure air of God's ways of thinking and feeling. It is a salvation that makes the heart pure, with the will and choice of the heart to be pure.

(SIII, 132–33)

206. Jesus did not die to save us from punishment; He was called Jesus because He should save His people from their sins.

(SIII, 133)

207. To recognize that we are to blame, is to say that we ought to be better, that we are able to do right if we will. We are able to turn our faces to the light, and come out of the darkness; the Lord will see to our growth.

(SIII, 190)

208. Yea, the fear of God will cause a man to flee, not from Him, but from himself; not from Him, but to Him, the Father of himself, in terror lest he should do Him wrong or his neighbour wrong.

(SI, 32)

209. To make a man happy as a lark, *might be* to do him grievous wrong; to make a man wake, rise, look up, turn, is worth the life and death of the Son of the Eternal.

(SII, 26)

210. We must become as little children, and Christ must be born in us; we must learn of Him, and the one lesson He has to give is Himself: He does first all He wants us to do; He is first all He wants us to be. We must not merely do as He did; we must see things as He saw them, regard them as He regarded them; we must take the will of God as the very life of our being; we must neither try to get our own way,

nor trouble ourselves as to what may be thought or said of us. The world must be to us as nothing.

(SII, 210–11)

211. It now ought not to be possible to mistake a Christian for a man of the world. His very dealings with every man that comes near him have something to show, something that Christ would have done that a man of the world would not do. Tell me how you would like Christ to come in upon you at any moment in the midst of your business talk. Would you be ready to turn to him and say, "Master, this is how I am saying the thing to my friend; this is how I see it in the light of Thy love." Would you be ready for that, or do you think a great part of your being and your life can be conducted upon other laws than Christian?

(GW, 122)

212. So, teaching him only that which she loved, not that which she had been taught, Janet read to Gibbie of Jesus, talked to him of Jesus, dreamed to him about Jesus; until at length—Gibbie did not think to watch, and knew nothing of the process by which it came about—his whole soul was full of the Man, of His doings, of His words, of His life. Jesus Christ was in him—he was possessed by Him. Almost before he knew, he was trying to fashion his life after that of his Master.

(SG, 152)

213. "Mr. Graham, how is it that you know there is a God, and one—one—fit to be trusted as you trust Him?"

"In no way that I can bring to bear on the reason of another so as to produce conviction."

"Then what is to become of me?"

"I can do for you what is far better. I can persuade you to look and see whether before your own door stands not a gate—lies not a path to walk in. Entering by that gate, walking in that path, you shall yourself arrive at the conviction, which no man can give you, that there is a living Love and Truth at the heart of your being, and pervading all that surrounds you. The man who seeks the truth in any other manner will never find it.... I sought comfort from the unknown source of my life. He gave me to understand His Son, and so I understood Himself, knew that I came of God, and was comforted."

"But how do you know that it was not all a delusion—the product of your fervid imagination?"

"Not to mention the conviction which a truth beheld must carry with itself, and concerning which there can be no argument either with him who does or him who does not see it, this experience goes far with me.... namely, that all of my difficulties and confusions have gone on clearing themselves up ever since I set out to walk in that way. My consciousness of life is threefold what it was; my perception of what is lovely around me, and my delight in it, threefold; my power of understanding things and of ordering my way, threefold also; the same with my hope and my courage, my love to my kind, my power of forgiveness. In short, I cannot but believe that my whole being and its whole world are in process of rectification for me ... if I thus find my whole being enlightened and redeemed ... if I find that His word and the result of action founded upon that word, correspond and agree ... am I likely to doubt much or long whether there be such a Lord or no?"

(ML, 254–55)

214. (Joseph Polwarth is a midget with a deformed body, and in the following four passages is his testimony. In the first, he becomes aware of his spiritual need.)

I began to be aware that, heavy affliction as it was to be made so different from my fellows, my outward deformity was but a picture of my inward condition. There nothing was right. Many things which in theory I condemned, and in others, despised were yet a part of myself, or, at best, part of an evil disease cleaving fast unto me. I found myself envious and revengeful and conceited. I discovered that I

looked down on people whom I thought less clever than
myself. . . .

All at once one day, with a sickening conviction it
came upon me . . . what a contemptible little wretch I was,
and writhed in the bright agony of conscious worthless-
ness.

I now concluded that I had been nothing but a Phari-
see and a hypocrite, praying with a bad heart, and that God
saw me just as detestable as I saw myself, and despised me
and was angry with me. I read my Bible more diligently
than ever for a time, found in it nothing but denunciation
and wrath, and soon dropped it in despair. I had already
ceased to pray.

(TW, 84–85)

215. (The following incident shows Joseph how he may
have misunderstood God.)

One day a little boy mocked me. I flew into a rage,
and, rendered by passion for the moment fleet and strong,
pursued and caught him. . . . When the boy found himself in
my clutches, he turned on me a look of such terror that it
disarmed me at once, and, confounded and distressed to
see a human being in such abject fear, a state which in my
own experience I knew to be horrible, . . . I would have let
him go instantly, but that I could not without having comforted him. But not a word of mine could get into his ears,
and I saw at length that he was so *pre*-possessed, that every
tone of kindness I uttered sounded to him a threat: nothing
would do but let him go. The moment he found himself
free, he fled headlong into the pond, got out again, ran
home, and told, with perfect truthfulness I believe, though
absolute inaccuracy, that I threw him in. After this I tried to
govern my temper, but found that the more I tried, the
more even that I succeeded outwardly, that is, succeeded in
suppressing the signs and deeds of wrath, the less could I
keep down the wrath in my soul. . . .

One evening, in the twilight, I lay alone in my little
den, not thinking, but with mind surrendered and passive to

what might come into it. It was very hot—indeed sultry. My
little skylight was open, but not a breath of air entered.
What preceded I do not know, but the face of the terrified
boy rose before me, or in me rather, and all at once I found
myself, eagerly, painfully, at length almost in an agony, per-
suading him that I would not hurt him, but meant well and
friendly towards him. Again I had just let him go in despair,
when the sweetest, gentlest, most refreshing little waft of
air came in at the window and just went *being,* hardly
moving, over my forehead. Its greeting was more delicate
than even my mother's kiss, and yet it cooled my whole
body. Now whatever, or whencesoever the link. . . . the next
thought of which I was aware was, What if I misunderstood
God the same way the boy had misunderstood me! and the
next thing was to take my New Testament from the shelf on
which I had laid it aside.

(TW, 85–86)

216. (He now studies the Bible.)
    Another evening of that same summer, I said to myself
that I would begin at the beginning and read [the Bible]
through. I had no definite idea in the resolve; it seemed a
good thing to do, and I would do it. It would serve towards
keeping up my connection in a way with *things above.* I
began, but did not that night get through the first chapter of
St. Matthew. Conscientiously I read every word of the gene-
alogy, but when I came to the twenty-third and read, "Thou
shalt call His name JESUS; *for He shall save His people from
their sins,"* I did not for a moment imagine that to be saved
from my sins meant to be saved from the punishment of
them. That would have been no glad tidings to me. My
sinfulness was ever before me, and often my sins too, and I
loved them not, yet could not free myself of them. They
were in me and of me, and how was I to part myself from
that which came to me with my consciousness, which asserted itself in me as one with my consciousness? I could
not get behind myself so as to reach its root. But here was
news of one who came from behind that root itself to deliv-

er me from that in me which made being a bad thing!

(TW, 86–87)

217. (Here is the conclusion of Joseph's testimony.)

"To tell you all that followed, if I could recall and narrate it in order, would take hours. Suffice it that from that moment I was a student, a disciple. Soon to me also came then the two questions: *How do I know that there is a God at all?* and *How am I to know that such a Man as Jesus ever lived?* I could answer neither. But in the meantime I was reading the story—was drawn to the Man there presented, and was trying to understand His being, and character, and principles of life and action. And to sum all in a word, many months had not passed ere I had forgotten to seek an answer to either question: they were in fact questions no longer: I had seen the Man Jesus Christ, and in Him had known the Father of Him and of me. My dear sir, no conviction can be got, or if it could be got, would be of any sufficing value, through that dealer in second-hand goods, the intellect. If by it we could prove there is a God, it would be of small avail indeed: we must see Him and know Him, to know that He was not a demon. But I know no other way of knowing that there is a God but that which reveals *what* He is—the only idea that could be God—shows Him in His own self-proving existence—and that way is Jesus Christ as He revealed Himself on earth, and as He is revealed afresh to every heart that seeks to know the truth concerning Him."

A pause followed—a solemn one—and then again Polwarth spoke.

"Either the whole frame of existence," he said, "is a wretched, miserable unfitness, a chaos with dreams of a world, a chaos in which the higher is for ever subject to the lower, or it is an embodied idea growing towards perfection in Him who is the one perfect creative Idea, the Father of lights who suffers Himself that He may bring His many sons into the glory which is His own glory."

(TW, 87–88)

218. (The remaining passages in this section outline the process of the new or second birth of one man. Thomas Wingfold, although a curate, is not a Christian. It begins when he is challenged by an atheist and realizes that he really does not know if Christianity is true. However, he now finds that he has a sincere desire to know the truth.)

If we could arrive at the feelings of a fish of the northern ocean around which the waters suddenly rose to tropical temperature, and swarmed with strange forms of life, uncouth and threatening, we should have a fair symbol of the mental condition in which Thomas Wingfold now found himself. The spiritual fluid in which his being floated had become all at once more potent, and he was in consequence uncomfortable. A certain intermittent stinging, as if from the flashes of some moral electricity, had begun to pass in various directions through the crude and chaotic mass he called himself, and he felt strangely restless. It never occurred to him—as how should it?—that he might have commenced undergoing the most marvellous of all changes,—one so marvellous indeed, that for a man to foreknow its result or understand what he was passing through, would be more strange than that a caterpillar should recognize in the rainbow-winged butterfly hovering over the flower at whose leaf he was gnawing the perfected idea of his own potential self—I mean the change of being born again. Nor were the symptoms such as would necessarily have suggested, even to a man experienced in the natural history of the infinite, that the process had commenced.

(TW, 50)

219. (Some good advice is given to Thomas.)

Take then your New Testament as if you had never seen it before, and read—to find out. If in Him [Jesus] you fail to meet God, then go to your consciousness of the race, your metaphysics, your Plato, your Spinoza. Till then this point remains: there was a Man who said He knew Him, and that if you would give heed to Him you too should know Him. The record left of Him is indeed scanty, yet enough to disclose what manner of Man He was—His principles, His way of looking at things, His thoughts of His Father and His brethren and the relations between them, of man's business in life, his destiny, and his hopes.

(TW, 90)

220. (Part of the process is the curate's service to those in need.)

The tenderness of the curate's service, the heart that showed itself in everything he did, even in the turn and expression of the ministering hand. . . . For while his intellect was hanging about the door, asking questions, and uneasily shifting hither and thither in its unloved perplexities, the spirit of the Master had gone by it unseen, and entered into the chamber of his heart.

(TW, 374)

221. On the stone he now seated himself, and fell a-musing.

What a change had come upon him—slow indeed, yet how vast—since the night when he sat in the same church-yard indignant and uneasy, with the words of Bascombe like hot coals in his heart! He had been made ashamed of himself who had never thought much of himself, but the more he had lost of worthiness in his own eyes, the more he had gained in worth; and the more his poor satisfaction with himself had died out, the more the world had awaked around him. For it must be remembered that a little conceit is no more to be endured than a great one, but must be swept utterly away. Sky and wind and water and birds and trees said to him, "Forget thyself, and we will think of thee. Sing no more to thyself thy foolish songs of decay, and we will all sing to thee of love and hope and faith and resurrection."

(TW, 330)

222. (As one indication of his changed life, Thomas finds himself more in tune with nature. However, MacDonald then describes the most important change.)

It was this: that whereas in former times the name Christ had been to him little more than a dull theological symbol, the thought of Him and His thoughts was now constantly with him; ever and anon some fresh light would break from the cloudy halo that enwrapped His grandeur; ever was He growing more the Son of Man to his loving heart, ever more the Son of God to his aspiring spirit. Testimony had merged almost in vision: he saw into, and partly understood, the perfection it presented: he looked upon the face of God and lived. Oftener and oftener, as the days passed, did it seem as if the Man were by his side, and at times, in the stillness of the summer eve, when he walked alone, it seemed almost, as thoughts of revealing arose in his heart, that the Master Himself was teaching him in spoken words. What need now to rack his soul in following the dim-seen, ever-vanishing paths of metaphysics? He had but to obey the Prophet of life, the Man whose being and doing and teaching were blended in one three-fold harmony—or, rather, were the three-fold analysis of one white essence— he had but to obey Him, haunt His footsteps, and harken after the sound of His spirit, and all truth would in healthy process be unfolded in himself. What philosophy could carry him where Jesus would carry His obedient friends—into His own peace, namely, far above all fear and all hate, where his soul should breathe such a high atmosphere of strength at once and repose, that he should love even his enemies, and that with no such love as condescendingly overlooks, but with the real, hearty, and self-involved affection that would die to give them the true life! Alas! How far was he from such perfection now—from such a martyrdom, lovely as endless, in the consuming fire of God! And at the thought, he fell from the heights of his contemplation—but was caught in the thicket of prayer.

(TW, 331)

223. He was gradually learning that his faith must be an absolute one, claiming from God everything the love of a perfect Father could give, or the needs He had created in

His child could desire; that he must not look to himself first for help, or imagine that the divine was only the supplement to the weakness and failure of the human; that the highest effort of the human was to lay hold of the divine. He learned that he could keep no simplest law in its loveliness until he was possessed of the same spirit whence that law sprung; that he could not even love Helen aright, simply, perfectly, unselfishly, except through the presence of the originating Love; that the one thing wherein he might imitate the creative will of God was, to will the presence and power of that will which gave birth to his. It was the vital growth of this faith even when he was too much troubled to recognize the fact that made him strong in the midst of weakness; when the Son of Man cried out "Let this cup pass," the Son of God in Him could yet cry "Let Thy will be done." He could inhabit trembling and yet be brave.

(TW, 442)

224. Alone in the dusky church the curate's [prayer] ascended like a song of the angels, for his heart was all a thanksgiving—not for any perfected gift, but for many a lovely hope. He knelt down by the organ and worshipped the God and Father of the Lord Jesus Christ—that God and no other was the God of his expectation. When he rose from his knees, the church was dark, but through the windows of the clerestory, many stars were shining.

(TW, 510)

SIX

 PRAYER

225. If, seeing we live not by our own will, we live by another will, then is there reason, and then only can there be reason in prayer.

(SII, 62)

226. He does not care to give anything but His best, or that which will prepare for it. Not many years may pass before you confess, "Thou art a God who hears prayer, and gives a better answer." You may come to see that the desire of your deepest heart would have been frustrated by having what seemed its embodiment then. That God should as a loving father listen, hear, consider, and deal with the request after the perfect tenderness of his heart, is to me enough; for it is little that I should go without what I pray for. If it be granted that any answer which did not come of love, and was not for the final satisfaction of him who prayed, would be unworthy of God; that it is the part of love and knowledge to watch over the wayward, ignorant child; then the trouble of seemingly unanswered prayers begins to abate, and a lovely hope and comfort takes its place in

the child-like soul. To hear is not necessarily to attend to—
sometimes as necessarily to refuse.

(SII, 71)

227. What if the main object in God's idea of prayer be the
supplying of our great, our endless need—the need of Himself? What if the good of all our smaller and lower needs
lies in this, that they help to drive us to God? Hunger may
drive the runaway child home, and he may or may not be
fed at once, but he needs his mother more than his dinner.
Communion with God is the one need of the soul beyond
all other need; prayer is the beginning of that communion,
and some need is the motive of that prayer. Our wants are
for the sake of our coming into communion with God, our
eternal need.

(SII, 72)

228. Every gift of God is but a harbinger of His greatest and
only sufficing gift—that of Himself. No gift unrecognized as
coming from God is at its own best; therefore many things
that God would gladly give us, things even that we need
because we are, must wait until we ask for them, that we
may know whence they come: when in all gifts we find Him,
then in Him we shall find all things.

(SII, 74)

229. ... for God to give a man because he asked for it that
which was not in harmony with His laws of truth and right,
would be to damn him—to cast him into outer darkness.

(SI, 25)

230. It is not love that grants a boon unwillingly; still less is
it love that answers a prayer to the wrong and hurt of him
who prays. Love is one, and love is changeless.

(SI, 27)

231. Say to Him: "My God, I am very dull and low and hard;
but Thou art wise and high and tender, and Thou art my

God. I am Thy child. Forsake me not." Then fold the arms of thy faith, and wait in quietness until light goes up in thy darkness. Fold the arms of thy faith I say, but not of thy action: bethink thee of something that thou oughtest to do, and go and do it, if it be but the sweeping of a room, or the preparing of a meal, or a visit to a friend. Heed not thy feelings: Do thy work.

(SI, 177–78)

232. Where we do that we ought not, and could have helped it, be moved to anger against us, O Christ! Do not treat us as if we were not worth being displeased with; let not our faults pass as if they were of no weight. Be angry with us, holy Brother, wherein we are to blame; where we do not understand, have patience with us, and open our eyes, and give us strength to obey, until at length we are the children of the Father even as Thou.

(SIII, 191)

233. (An orphan girl whose bedroom is in an attic is frightened of rats.)

"O God, keep me safe from the rats."

There was no need to send an angel from heaven in answer to this little one's prayer: the cat would do. Annie heard a scratch and a mew at the door. The rats made one frantic scramble, and were still. . . .

Fortified by the cat's arrival, and still more by the feeling that it was a divine messenger sent to succor her because she had prayed, she sprang out of bed, darted across the room, and opened the door to let her in. A few moments and she was fast asleep, guarded by God's angel, the cat, for whose entrance she took good care ever after to leave the door ajar.

There are ways of keeping the door of the mind also, ready as it is to fall to, ajar for the cat.

(AF*, 25)

———

*Indicates translation of Scottish into English.

234. (After Simon complains about possible flood damage to his mill, Thomas advises him to pray about it.)

"Pray to God about an old meal-mill?" said Simon with indignation. "Indeed, I will not be so ill-bred."

And so saying, he turned and went home leaving Thomas muttering—

"If a body would pray about anything, they might, maybe take a liking to it. A prayer may do a body good when it's not quite the kind to be altogether acceptable to the mind of the Almighty. But I doubt that His ear is closed for any prayer that goes up His way."

(AF*, 284)

235. (With cross words, Thomas sends a friend away so that he can pray alone.)

But the secret place of the Most High will not be entered after this fashion; and Thomas felt that he was shut out. It is not by driving away our brother that we can be alone with God. . . . In such a mood, the chamber with the shut door shuts out God too, and one is left alone with himself, which is the outer darkness. The love of the brethren opens the door into God's chamber.

(AF, 204–5)

236. The fact was, my uncle, amongst his other peculiarities, did not approve of teaching children to say their prayers. But he did not therefore leave me without instruction in the matter of praying—either the idlest or the most availing of human actions. He would say, "When you want anything, ask for it, Willie; and if it is worth your having, you will have it. But don't fancy you are doing God any service by praying to Him. He likes you to pray to Him because He loves you, and wants you to love Him. And whatever you do, don't go saying a lot of words you don't mean. If you think you ought to pray, say your Lord's Prayer and be done with it."

(WC, 149–50)

---

*Indicates translation of Scottish into English.

237. (A grandfather's concern for his wayward granddaughter leads to the following comments.)

It's very true that we haven't that much weight with her, for it seems a kind of law of nature that the young's not to be held down by the experience of the old—which after all, can be experience only to themselves. But when we pray to God, it seems it puts it in God's power to make use of us for the carrying out of the thing we pray for; we don't know how, but so it seems to be; and God can work through us without our knowing how. It's not always by the words He gives us to say; with some folk words go for uncommon little; it may be sometimes by a look of which you know nothing yourself; or it may be sometimes by a move of your hand, or a turn of your voice or your head, where no attention is paid to the word you say. Who knows but you may have a divine power over the heart you have almost given up the hope of winning. . . . There's no knowing what God can do nor yet what best of reasons He has for not doing it sooner! When we think He's letting the time go by and doing nothing, He may just be doing all things. . . . I can but pray the Father of all to hold off the hardening of the heart that despises council. I really doubt that her grandmother and I can do much more for her. . . . We'll just lay our cares in the fine sight and the loving heart of the Master and see what He can do for us. He knows we must be concerned about such things! But even such we can leave to Him! He'll maybe let us see something we should do, or maybe do the necessary thing without using us.

(DG*, 226)

238. "Come, my child . . . let us kneel down here on the grass and pray to God who is in yon star just twinkling through the tray, and in my heart and in yours, my child."

I will not give the words of the minister's prayer. The words are not the prayer. Mr. Drake's words were common-

---

*Indicates translation of Scottish dialect into English.

place, with much of the conventionality and the platitude of
prayer-meetings. He had always objected to the formality of
the Prayer-book, but the words of his own prayers without
book was far more formal; the prayer itself was in the heart,
not on the lips, and was far better than the words.

(PF, 161–62)

239. She had come nearly to the point of discovering that
the soul is not capable of generating its own requirements,
that it needs to be supplied from a well whose springs lie
deeper than its own soil, in the infinite All, namely, upon
which that soil rests. Happy they who have found that those
springs have an outlet in their hearts—on the hill of prayer.

(TW, 185)

240. Not only did Janet often pray with Gibbie, but sometimes as she read, her heart would grow so full, her soul be
so pervaded with conviction, perhaps the consciousness, of
the presence of the Man who had said He would be always
with His friends, that, sitting there on her stool, she would
begin talking to Him out of the very depths of her
life. ... Then would Gibbie listen indeed, awed by very
gladness. He never doubted that Jesus was there, or that
Janet saw Him all the time although he could not.

This custom of praying aloud, she had grown into so
long before Gibbie came to her. ... It came in part from the
intense reality of her belief, and was in part a willed foster-
ing of its intensity. She never imagined that words were
necessary; she believed that God knew her every thought,
and that the moment she lifted up her heart, it entered into
communion with Him; but the very sound of the words she
spoke seemed to make her feel nearer to the Man who
being the eternal Son of the Father, yet had ears to hear
and lips to speak, like herself. To talk to Him aloud, also
kept her thoughts together, helped her to feel the fact of the
things she contemplated as well as the reality of His
presence.

(SG, 178)

241. (A pastor's response to a parishioner's comment.)
" ... But His will be done."

"Amen. There is no prayer in the universe as that. It means everything best and most beautiful. Thy will, O God, evermore be done."

(AN, 494)

242. (A young man, who has a very difficult duty to perform, has the following conversation with his spiritual adviser.)

"I hope it isn't wrong to wish it over, Mr. Polwarth?"

"I don't think it is wrong to wish anything you can talk to Him about and submit to His will. St. Paul says, 'In every thing let your requests be made known unto God.'"

"I sometimes feel as if I would not ask Him for anything, but just let Him give me what He likes...."

"Not to ask may seem to you a more submissive way, but I don't think it is so childlike. It seems to me far better to say, 'O Lord, I should like this or that, but I would rather not have it, if Thou dost not like it also.' Such prayer brings us into conscious and immediate relations with God. Remember, our thoughts are then passing to Him, sent by our will into His mind. Our Lord taught us to pray always and not get tired of it. God, however poor creatures we may be, would have us talk to Him, for then He can speak to us better than when we turn no face to Him."

(TW, 448–89)

243. We must never fear the will of God, Alister! We are not right until we can pray heartily, not say submissively, "Thy will be done." We have not one interest and God another. When we wish what He does not wish, we are not more against Him than against our real selves. We are traitors to the human when we think anything but the will of God desirable.

(WM, 246–47)

244. (Following is a prayer for a lady who is experiencing severe trials with intense mental anguish.)

Life eternal, this lady of Thine hath a sore heart and we cannot help her. Thou art Help, O mighty love. They who know Thee best rejoice in Thee most. As Thy sun that shines over our heads, as Thy air that flows unto our bodies, Thou art above, around, and in us; Thou art in her heart; oh, speak to her there; let her know Thy will, and give her strength to do it, O Father of Jesus Christ! Amen.

(TW, 259)

245. (A beautiful young lady in great suffering is staying with two people who are physically deformed but spiritually beautiful.)

At first when she found they had no set prayers in the house, she concluded that . . . they were not very religious. But by and by she began to discover that no one could tell when they might not be praying. At the most unexpected times she would hear her host's voice uttering tones of glad beseeching, or out-poured adoration. One day, when she had a bad headache, the little man came into her room, and, without a word to her, kneeled by her bedside, and said, "Father, who through Thy Son knowest pain, and Who dost even now in Thyself feel the pain of this Thy child, help her to endure until Thou shalt say it is enough, and send it from her. Let it not overmaster her patience; let it not be too much for her. What good it shall work in her, Thou, Lord, needest not that we should instruct Thee." Thereupon he rose and left the room.

(PF, 366)

246. (Two midgets with deformed bodies who live with much physical pain are yet devout Christians and one of them prays the following prayer.)

O Father of life, we praise Thee that one day Thou will take Thy poor crooked creatures, and give them bodies like Christ's, perfect as His, and full of Thy light. Help us to grow faster—as fast as Thou canst help us grow. Help us to keep

our eyes on the opening of Thy hand, that we may know the
manna when it comes. O Lord, we rejoice that we are Thy
making, though Thy handiwork is not very clear in the outer man as yet. We bless Thee that we feel Thy hand making
us. What if it be in pain! Evermore we hear the voice of the
Potter above the human grind of His wheel. Father, Thou
only knowest how we love Thee. Fashion the clay to Thy
beautiful will. To the eyes of men we are vessels of dishon-
or, but we know Thou dost not despise us, for Thou has
made us, and Thou dwellest with us. Thou has made us
love Thee, and hope in Thee, and in Thy love we will be
brave and endure. All in good time, O Lord. Amen.

(PF, 316)

247. (The following is a prayer by a young man said to be
simple or half-witted. The Bonny Man is his name for
Christ.)

Bonny Man, I know You well. There's no one in heaven
or earth that's like You. You know Yourself that I would just
die for You; or if there be anything worse to endure than
dying, that's what I would do for You—if You wanted it of
me, that is, for I'm hoping much that You will not want it,
I'm that awful cowardly! Oh Bonny Man, take the fear out of
my heart, and make me ready just to walk off of the face of
the world to do Your will, without thinking twice about it.
And oh, Bonny Man, won't You come down sometime before long and walk the hill here, that I may look upon You
once more—as in the days of old, when the starlit mountain shook with the might of the prayer You heaved up to
Your Father in heaven. . . . And oh, Bonny Man, give a look
in the face of my father and mother in their bed; and I pray
You see that [my sister] Kirsty's getting a fine sleep for she
has a heap of trouble with me: she is worth minding!—and
that clever!—as You know who made her! And look upon
this little house that I call my own, and they all helped me
to build, but as a lean-to to the house at home, for I'm not
away from it or them—just as that house and this house
and all houses are all nothing but children's houses built by

themselves about the floor of Your kitchen and in the nooks of the same—Your own timber and stones and thatch, Sir.

(HS*, 102–3)

248. "When do you go?"
"Tomorrow morning—as I propose."
"Then God be with thee. He *is* with thee, only my prayer is that thou mayest know it."

(ML, 306)

249. (During a terrible flood, Robert and Janet do not know where their foster son is.)

Robert had kept on going to the barn, and back again to the kitchen, all the morning, consumed with anxiety about the son of his old age; but the barn began to be flooded, and he had to limit his prayer-walk to the space between the door of the house and the chair where Janet sat—knitting busily, and praying with countenance untroubled, amidst the rush of the seaward torrents [and] the mad howling and screeching of the wind. . . .

"O Lord," she said in her great trusting heart, "if my bonnie lad be drowning in the water or dying of cold on the hillside, hold his hand. Be not far from him, Oh Lord, do not let him be frightened."

To Janet, what we call life and death were comparatively small matters, but she was very tender over suffering and fear. She did not pray half so much for Gibbie's life as for the presence with him of Him who is at the deathbed of every sparrow. True, she was not his bodily mother, but she loved him far better than the mother who, in such a dread for her child, would have been mad with terror. The difference was, that Janet loved up as well as down, loved down so widely, so intensely, because the Lord of life who gives His own to us, was more to her than any child can be to any mother, and she knew that He could not forsake her

*Indicates translation of Scottish dialect into English.

Gibbie, and that His presence was more and better than life. She was unnatural, was she?—inhuman?—Yes, if there be no such heart and source of humanity as she believed in; if there be, then such calmness and courage and content as hers are the mere human and natural condition to be hungered after by every aspiring soul. Not until such condition is mine shall I be able to regard life as a godlike gift, except in the hope that it is drawing nigh. Let him who understands, understand better; let him not say the good is less than perfect, or excuse his supineness and spiritual sloth by saying to himself that a man can go too far in his search after the divine, can sell too much of what he has to buy the field of the treasure. Either there is no Christ of God, or my all is His.

(SG*, 229–30)

250. (A little girl is lost in the mountains.)
       ... When all at once a verse she had heard the Sunday before at church seemed to come of itself into her head: "Call upon Me in the time of trouble and I will answer thee." It must mean that she was to ask God to help her: was that the same as saying prayers? But she wasn't good and He wouldn't hear anybody that wasn't good. Then, if He was only the God of the good people, what was to become of the rest when they were lost on mountains? She had better try; it could not do much harm. Even if He would not hear her, He would not surely be angry with her for calling upon Him when she was in such trouble. So thinking, she began to pray to what dim distorted reflection of God there was in her mind. They alone pray to the real God, the Maker of the heart that prays, who knows His Son Jesus. If our prayers were heard only in accordance with the idea of God to which we seem to ourselves to pray, how miserable would our infinite wants be met! But every honest cry, even if sent into the deaf ear of an idol, passes on to the ears of the unknown God, the heart of the unknown Father.

(SG, 194)

---

*Indicates translation of Scottish dialect into English.

251. And if there was a good deal of superstition mingled with her prayer, the main thing in it was genuine that is, the love that prompted it; and if God heard only perfect prayers, how could He be the prayer-hearing God?

(WM, 33)

252. "Lady Emily," Margaret went on, "if I felt my heart as hard as a stone; if I did not love God, or man, or woman, or little child, I would yet say to God in my heart, 'O God, see how I trust Thee because Thou art perfect and not changeable like me. I do not love Thee. I love nobody. I am not even sorry for it. Thou seest how much I need Thee to come close to me, to put Thy arm round me, to say to me, *My child;* for the worse my state, the greater my need of my Father who loves me. Come to me, and my day will dawn. My beauty and my love will come back; and oh! how I shall love Thee, my God! and know that my love is Thy love, my blessedness Thy being.'"

(DE, 233–34)

253. (An elderly minister's doubts due to a period of adversity lead a minister-friend to pray with him.)

God of justice, Thou knowest how hard it is for us, and Thou wilt be fair to us. We have seen no visions; we have never heard the voice of Thy Son, of whom those tales, so dear to us, have come down the ages; we have to fight on in much darkness of spirit and of mind, both from the ignorance we cannot help, and from the fault we could have helped; we inherit blindness from the error of our fathers; and when fear, or the dread of shame, or the pains of death, come upon us like a wall, and Thou appearest nowhere, either in our hearts, or in the outer universe; we cannot tell whether the things we seemed to do in Thy name, were not mere hypocrisies, and our very life is but a gulf of darkness. We cry aloud, and our despair is as a fire in our bones to make us cry; but to all our crying and listening, there seems neither hearing nor answer in the boundless waste. Thou who knowest Thyself God, who knowest Thyself that for which we groan, Thou whom Jesus called Father, we appeal to Thee, not as we imagine Thee, but as Thou seest Thyself as Jesus knows Thee, to Thy very self we cry—help us, O Cause of us! O Thou from whom alone we are this weakness, through whom alone we can become strength, help us—be our Father. We ask for nothing beyond what Thy Son has told us to ask. We beg for no signs or wonders, but for Thy breath upon our souls. Thy spirit in our hearts. We pray for no cloven tongues of fire—for no mighty rousing of brain or imagination; but we do with all our power of prayer, pray for Thy spirit; we do not even pray to know that it is given to us; let us, if it so pleases Thee, remain in doubt of the gift for years to come—but lead us thereby. Knowing ourselves only as poor and feeble, aware only of ordinary and common movements of mind and soul, may we yet be possessed by the spirit of God, led by His will in ours. For all things in a man, even those that seem to him the commonest and least uplifted, are the creation of Thy heart, and by the lowly doors of our wavering judgment, dull imagination, lukewarm love, and palsied will, Thou canst enter and glorify all. Give us patience because our hope is in Thee, not in ourselves. Work Thy will in us, and our prayers are ended, Amen.

(PF, 129)

254. (A prayer by Kirsty, a young woman, after truthfully confronting a friend about his weaknesses and his need to face his responsibilities.)

"Lord I have done all I can. Until You have done some thing by Yourself, I can do nothing more. He's in Your hands still, I praise You, though he's out of mine! Lord if I have done him any ill forgive me; a poor human body cannot always know the best! Don't let him suffer for my ignorance, whether I'm to blame for it or not. I will try to do whatever Thou makest plain for me."

---

*Indicates translation of Scottish dialect into English.

(Unknown, at the time, to Kirsty, her friend's short prayer at about the same time was "God help me," and his life began anew.)

(HS*, 244)

255. Not for years had Janet been to church; she had long been unable to walk so far; and having no book but the best, and no help to understand it but the highest, her faith was simple, strong, real, all-pervading. Day by day she pored over the great gospel—I mean just the good news according to Matthew and Mark and Luke and John—until she had grown to be one of the noble ladies of the kingdom of heaven—one of those who inherit the earth, and are ripening to see God. For the Master, and His mind in hers, was her teacher. She had little or no theology save what He taught her, or rather, what He *is* . . . To know *Him* is to know God. And he only who obeys Him, does or can know Him; he who obeys Him cannot fail to know Him. To Janet, Jesus Christ was no object of so-called theological speculation, but a living Man, who somehow or other heard her when she called to Him, and sent her the help she needed.

(SG, 78)

 OBEDIENCE

256. The Lord cared neither for isolated truth nor for orphaned deed. It was truth in the inward parts, it was the good heart, the mother of good deeds, He cherished.

(SII, 6)

257. For the immediate end of the commandments never was that men should succeed in obeying them, but that, finding they could not do that which yet must be done, finding the more they tried the more was required of them, they should be driven to the source of life and law—of their life and His law—to seek from Him such reinforcement of life as should make the fulfillment of the law as possible, yea, as natural, as necessary.

(SII, 11)

258. Had he had more of the wisdom of the serpent . . . he would perhaps have known that to try too hard to make people good, is one way to make them worse; that the only way to make them good is to be good—remembering well the beam and the mote; that the time for speaking comes rarely, the time for being never departs.

(SG, 335)

259. Obedience is the one key of life.

(SII, 62)

260. Obedience is the one condition of progress. . . .

(DO, 289)

261. Obedience is the only service.

(MOL, 93)

262. Would that our pulpits were all in the power of such men as by suffering know the human, and by obedience the divine heart!

(TW, 373)

263. He then proceeded to show that faith and obedience are one and the same spirit, passing as it were, from room to room in the same heart: what in the heart we call faith, in the will we call obedience. He showed that the Lord refused absolutely the faith that found its vent at the lips in the worshipping words, and not at the limbs in obedient action—which some present pronounced bad theology, while others said to themselves surely that at least was common sense.

(TW, 152)

264. . . . Get up, and do something the master tells you; so make yourself His disciple at once. Instead of asking yourself whether you believe or not, ask yourself whether you have this day done one thing because He said, Do it, or once abstained because He said, Do not do it. It is simply absurd to say you believe, or even want to believe in Him, if you do not anything He tells you. If you can think of nothing He ever said as having had an atom of influence on your doing or not doing, you have too good ground to consider yourself no disciple of His.

(SII, 244–45)

265. Doubtless Gibbie, as well as many a wiser man, might now and then make a mistake in the embodiment of his obedience, but even where the action misses the command, it may yet be obedience to Him who gave the command, and by obeying one learns how to obey.

(SG, 334)

266. "Is not generosity something more than duty—something higher, something beyond it?"

"Yes," answered Malcolm, "so long as it does not go against duty, but keeps in the same direction, is in harmony with it. I doubt much, though, whether, as we grow in what is good, we shall not come soon to see that generosity is but our duty, and nothing very grand and beyond it."

(ML, 185)

267. It is not the ruling being who is most like God; it is the man who ministers to his fellow, who is like God; and the man who will just sternly and rigidly do what his master tells him ... who is likest Christ in that one particular matter.

(DO, 307)

268. O friends! It is the deed that stirs the man; it is the thing you do, and not what you feel. I have heard one of the best of men lamenting to me that sometimes it seemed to him as if he had no feeling at all ... but his hands and his heart were busy for his fellow-creatures from morning to night, and his prayer ascended to the God of his salvation. We were not meant to be creatures of feeling; we were meant to be creatures of conscience, first of all, and then of consciousness towards God—a sense of His presence; and if we go on, the feeling will come all right. Our feelings will blossom as a rose just from the very necessity of things.

(GW, 11)

269. But duty itself is only a stage toward something better. It is but the impulse, God given I believe, toward a far more

vital contact with the truth. We shall one day forget all about duty, and do everything from the love of the loveliness of it, the satisfaction of the rightness of it. What would you say to a man who ministered to the wants of his wife and family only from duty? Of course you wish heartily that the man who neglects them would do it from any cause, even were it fear of the whip; but the strongest and most operative sense of duty would not satisfy you in such a relation. There are depths of righteousness. Duty is the only path to freedom, but that freedom is the love that is beyond and prevents duty.

(PF, 206)

270. ... there is no such thing in the world as liberty, except under the law of liberty; that is, the acting according to the essential laws of our own being—not our feelings which go and come.

(GW, 28)

271. ... the one only liberty lies in obedience.

(GW, 29)

272. ... if we, choosing, against our liking, do the right, go on so until we are enabled by doing it to see into the very loveliness and essence of the right, and know it to be altogether beautiful, and then at last never think of doing evil, but delight with our whole souls in doing the will of God, why then, do you not see, we combine the two, and we are free indeed, because we are acting like God out of the essence of our nature, knowing good and evil, and choosing the good with our whole hearts and delighting in it?

(GW, 32–33)

273. A man may indeed have turned to obey God, and yet be capable of many an injustice to his neighbour which he has not yet discovered to be an injustice; but as he goes on obeying, he will go on discovering. ... A man who contin-

ues capable of a known injustice to his neighbour, cannot be believed to have turned to God.

(SIII, 217)

274. It is to the man who is trying to live, to the man who is obedient to the word of the Master, that the word of the Master unfolds itself.

(SII, 41)

275. Until we love the Lord so as to do what He tells us, we have no right to have an opinion about what one of those men [writers of the N.T. epistles] meant, for all they wrote about is about things beyond us. The simplest woman who tries not to judge her neighbor or not to be anxious for the morrow, will better know what is best to know than the best-read bishop without that one simple outgoing of his highest nature in the effort to do the will of Him who thus spoke.

(AN, 128)

276. "A thousand foolish doctrines may be unquestioned in the mind and never interfere with the growth or bliss of him who lives in active subordination of his life to the law of life: obedience will in time exorcise them, like many another worse devil."

(MM, 24)

277. "The only way to learn the rules of anything practical is to begin to do the thing. We have enough knowledge in us ... to begin anything requested of us. The sole way to deal with the profoundest mystery ... is to begin to do some duty revealed by (it). . . ."

"Yes, Yes! But how is one to know what is true my dear? There are so many differing claims to the quality!"

"I have been told and believe it with all my heart," replied Hester, "that the only way to know what is true is to do what is true."

"But you must know what is true before you can begin to do what is true."

"Everybody knows something that is true to do—that is, something he ought to lose no time in setting about. The true thing is the thing that must not be let alone but done. It is much easier to know what is true to do than what is true to think. But those who do the one will come to know the other—and none else, I believe."

(WW, 129, 373)

278. (While meditating on God's Word, a minister wonders how he can understand some of its difficult sayings.)

With this, yet another saying dawned upon him: *If any man will do His Will, He shall know of the doctrine, whether it be of God, or whether I speak of myself.*

He went into his closet and shut to the door: came out again, and went straight to visit a certain grievous old woman.

(TW, 149–50)

279. Whosoever . . . will do the will of God—not understand it, not care about it, not theorize it, but do it—is a son of God.

(GW, 126–27)

280. Oh the folly of any mind that would explain God before obeying Him! that would map out the character of God, instead of crying, Lord, what wouldst Thou have me to do?

(SIII, 115)

281. Our business is not to think correctly, but live truly; then first will there be a possibility of our thinking correctly. One chief cause of the amount of unbelief in the world is, that those who have seen something of the glory of Christ, set themselves to theorize concerning Him rather than to obey Him.

(SIII, 135)

282. Obey the truth, I say, and let theory wait. Theory may spring from life, but never life from theory.

(SIII, 152)

283. The greatest obscuration of the words of the Lord, as of all true teachers, comes from those who give themselves to interpret rather than do them. Theologians have done more to hide the gospel of Christ than any of its adversaries. It was not for our understandings, but our will, that Christ came. He who does that which he sees, shall understand; he who is set upon understanding rather than doing, shall go on stumbling and mistaking and speaking foolishness.

(SII, 98–99)

284. Had you given yourselves to the understanding of His word that you might do it, and not to the quarrying from it of material wherewith to buttress your systems, in many a heart by this time would the name of the Lord be loved where now it remains unknown.

(SII, 255)

285. ... our business is not to speculate what we would do in other circumstances, but to perform the duty of the moment, the one true preparation for the duty to come.

(EA, 227)

286. [He was] a godly man, who lived that which he could ill explain, and was immeasurably better than those parts of his creed which from a sense of duty, he pushed to the front.

(WM, 23)

287. ... she heard much religious conversation.... She thus became familiar with the forms of a religious belief as narrow as its partisans are numerous.... She never questioned the truth of what she heard, and became skilled in its idioms and arguments and forms of thought. But the

more familiar one becomes with any religious system, while yet the conscience and will are unawakened and obedience has not begun, the harder it is to enter into the kingdom of heaven. Such familiarity is a soul-killing experience.

(PF, 96)

288. (Gilbert is an orphan boy who is trying to follow the teachings of Jesus. His guardians, a minister and his wife, are baffled by this.)
The idea of anybody ordering his common doings ... by principles drawn from a source far too sacred to be practically regarded, was too preposterous to have ever become even a notion to her....
"You really must, Mr. Sclater, teach him the absurdity of attempting to fit every point of his behavior to—to—words which were of course quite suitable to the time when they were spoken, but which it is impossible to take literally nowadays." ... In obedience to his wife, Mr. Sclater did what he could to show Sir Gilbert how mistaken he was in imagining he could fit his actions to the words of our Lord. Shocked as even he would probably have been at such a characterization of his attempt, it amounted practically to this: Do not waste your powers in the endeavor to keep the commandments of our Lord, for it cannot be done, and He knew it could not be done and never meant it should be done. He pointed out to him, not altogether unfairly, the difficulties, and the causes of mistake, with regard to the words; but said nothing to reveal the spirit and life of them.

(SG, 308, 316, 334)

289. Others again judged him a fanatic—a dangerous man ... what man was more dangerous than he who went too far? Possibly these forgot that the narrow way can hardly be one to sit down in comfortably, or indeed be entered at all save by him who tries the gate with the intent of going all the way—even should it lead up to the perfection of the father in heaven. "But," they would in effect have argued, "is not a fanatic dangerous? And is not an enthusi-

ast always in peril of becoming a fanatic?" Be his enthusi-
asm for what it may—for Jesus Christ, for God Himself—
such a man is dangerous, most dangerous.

(TW, 188)

290. Middling good people are shocked at the wickedness
of the wicked; Gibbie, who knew both so well, and what
ought to be expected, was shocked only at the wickedness
of the righteous.

(SG, 289)

291. Whatever interpretation we put on [Pilate's treatment
of Christ], he must be far less worthy of blame than those
"Christians" who, instead of setting themselves to be pure
"even as He is pure," to be their brother and sister's keeper,
and to serve God by being honourable in shop and count-
ing-house and labour-market, proceed to "serve" Him,
some by going to church or chapel, some by condemning
the opinions of their neighbours, some by teaching others
what they do not themselves heed.

(SIII, 101)

292. A curious halo began to shimmer about the heads of
the young men in the picture-gallery of the girl's fancy. Not
the less, however, did they regard them as enthusiasts, unfitted to this world, incapable of self-protection, too good to
live—in a word unpractical! Because a man would live according to the laws of his being as well as his body, obeying
simple, imperative, essential human necessity, his fellows
forsooth call him *unpractical!* Of the idiotic delusions of the
children of this world, that of being practical is one of the
most ludicrous.

(WM, 196)

293. (The following passage describes the beliefs of a lady
concerning the importance of doctrine.)
  Homage to will and word of the Master, apart from the
acceptance of certain doctrines concerning Him, was in her

eyes not merely defective but dangerous. To love the Lord with the love of truest obedience; to believe Him the Son of God and the saver of men with absolute acceptance of the heart was far from enough! It was but sentimental affection!

A certain young preacher in Scotland some years ago, accused by an old lady of preaching works, took refuge in the Lord's sermon on the mount: "Ow aye!" answered the partisan, "but He was a very young Man when He preached that sermon!"

(WM*, 61)

294. Obedience is the grandest thing in the world to begin with. Yes, and we shall end with it too. I do not think the time will ever come when we shall not have something to do, because we are told to do it without knowing why.

(DO, 307)

295. Those parents act foolishly who wish to explain every-thing to their children—most foolishly. No; teach your child to obey, and you give him the most precious lesson that can be given to a child.

(DO, 307)

296. Diamond learned to drive all the sooner that he had been accustomed to do what he was told, and could obey the smallest hint in a moment. Nothing helps one to get on like that. Some people don't know how to do what they are told; they have not been used to it, and they neither under-stand quickly nor are able to turn what they do understand into action quickly. With an obedient mind one learns the rights of things fast enough; for it is the law of the universe, and to obey is to understand.

(AB, 175)

297. As he thought and thought, it became gradually plainer that he must begin his obedience by getting ready

---

*Indicates translation of Scottish dialect into English.

for anything that God might require of him. Therefore he must go on learning till the call came.

(RF, 366)

298. We must learn to obey Him in everything, and so must begin somewhere: let it be at once, and in the very next thing that lies at the door of our conscience! Oh fools and slow of heart, if you think of nothing but Christ, and do not set yourselves to do His words! you but build your houses on the sand.

(SII, 245)

299. What he *can* judge of is, his duty at a given moment—and that not in the abstract, but as something to be by him *done,* neither more, nor less, nor other than *done.*

(DO, 73)

300. . . . to say a man might disobey and be none the worse, would be to say that *no* may be *yes,* and light sometimes darkness; it would be to say that the will of God is not man's bliss.

(SIII, 192)

301. She knew that she ought to be good, and she knew she was not good; how to be good she did not know, for she had never set herself to be good. She sometimes wished she were good; but there are thousands of wandering ghosts who would be good if they might without taking trouble: the kind of goodness they desire would not be worth a life to hold it.

(WM, 78)

302. How many people would like to be good, if only they might be made good without taking trouble about it! They do not like goodness well enough to hunger and thirst after it, or to sell all that they have that they may buy it; they will not falter at the gate of the kingdom of heaven; but they look with pleasure on this or that aerial castle of righteous-

ness, and think it would be rather nice to live in! They do not know that it is goodness all the time that their very being is pining after, and that they are starving their nature of its necessary food.

(PF, 298)

303. We are very ready to draw in our minds a distinction between respectable sins—human imperfections we call them, perhaps—and disreputable vices, such as theft and murder; but there is no such distinction in fact. Many a thief is a better man than many a clergyman, and miles nearer to the gates of the kingdom. The heavenly order goes upon other principles than ours, and there are first that shall be last and last that shall be first. Only, at the root of all human bliss lies repentance.

(TW, 341)

304. As one standing on the outskirts of a listening Galilean crowd, a word comes now and then to my hungry ears and hungrier heart: I turn and tell it again to you—not that ye have not heard it also, but that I may stir you up to ask yourselves: "Do I then obey this word? Have I ever, have I once sought to obey it? Am I a pupil of Jesus? Am I a Christian?" Hear then of His words. For me, they fill my heart with doubt and dismay.

The Lord says, *Love your enemies.* Sayest thou, *It is impossible.* Then dost thou mock the word of Him who said, *I am the Truth,* and hast no part in Him. Sayest thou, *Alas! I cannot?* Thou sayest true, I doubt not. But hast thou tried whether He who made will not increase the strength put forth to obey Him? . . .

The Lord said, *All things whatsoever ye would that men should do to you do ye even so to them.* Ye that buy and sell, do you obey this law? Examine yourselves and see. Ye would that men should deal fairly by you: do you deal fairly by them as ye would count fairness in them to you? If conscience makes you hang the head inwardly however you sit with it erect in the pew, dare you add to your crime against the law and the prophets the insult to Christ of calling yourself His disciple?

Not every one that sayeth to Me Lord, Lord, shall enter into the kingdom of heaven, but he that doeth the will of My Father which is in heaven.

(TW, 179–81)

305. (In a dream, a man searches for the original manuscript of the Gospel of John and finally finds it.)

On the table was a closed book. Oh! How my heart beat. . . . What doubts and fears would not this one lovely, oh! unutterably beloved volume, lay at rest for ever! . . . Nearly eighteen hundred years—and there it lay!—and there *was* a man who *did* hear the Master say the words and did set them down! . . . At last with sudden daring, I made a step towards the table, and bending with awe, out-stretched my hand to lay it on the book. But ere my hand reached it, another hand, from the opposite side of the table, appeared upon it—an old blue-veined, but powerful hand. I looked up. There stood the beloved disciple! His countenance was as a mirror from which shone back the face of the Master. Slowly he lifted the book, and turned away. Then first I saw behind him as it were an altar where-on a fire of wood was burning, and a pang of dismay shot to my heart, for I knew what he was about to do. He laid the book on the burning wood, and regarded it with a smile as it shrunk and shriveled and smouldered to ashes. Then he turned to me and said, while a perfect heaven of peace shone in his eyes: "Son of man, the Word of God liveth and abideth for ever, not in the volume of the book, but in the heart of the man that in love obeyeth Him." And therewith I awoke weeping, but with the lesson of my dream.

(TW, 175)

EIGHT

 POSSESSIONS

306. Things go wrong because men have such absurd and impossible notions about *possession*. They are always trying to possess, to call their own, things which it is impossible from their very nature, ever to possess or make their own.

(DG, 77)

307. The man who for consciousness of well-being depends upon any thing but life, the life essential, is a slave; he hangs on what is less than himself. He is not perfect who, deprived of every *thing*, would not sit down calmly content, aware of a well-being untouched; for none the less would he be possessor of all things, the child of the Eternal.

(SII, 35)

308. If we are the Lord's we possess the kingdom of heaven, and so inherit the earth. How many who call themselves by His name, would have it otherwise: they would possess the earth and inherit the kingdom! Such fill churches and chapels on Sundays: anywhere suits for the worship of Mammon.

(HG, 95)

309. Gibbie had not been educated in the relative grandeur of things of this world, and he regarded the things he now saw just as things, without the smallest notion of any power in them to confer superiority by being possessed.... Gibbie was incapable even of the notion that they mattered a straw to the life of any man. Indeed, to compare man with man was no habit of his; hence it cannot be wonderful that stone hearth and steel grate, clay floor and Brussels carpet were much the same to him. Man was the one sacred thing.

(SG, 280)

310. No amount of wealth sets one free from the obligation to work—in a world the God of which is ever working. He who works not has not yet discovered what God made him for, and is a false note in the orchestra of the universe. The possession of wealth is as it were pre-payment, and involves an obligation of honour to the doing of correspondent work. He who does not know what to do has never seriously asked himself what he ought to do.

(MOL, 59–60)

311. Wherein is the life of that man who merely does his eating and drinking and clothing after a civilized fashion better than that of the gypsy or tramp? If the civilized man is honest to boot, and gives good work in return for the bread or turtle on which he dines and the gypsy, on the other hand, steals his dinner, I recognize the importance of the difference; but if the rich man plunders the community by exorbitant profits, or speculation with other people's money, while the gypsy adds a fowl or two to the product of his tinkering; or, once again, if the gypsy is honest as the honest citizen, which is not so rare a case by any means as people imagine, I return to my question: Wherein, I say, are the warm house, the windows hung with purple, and the table covered with fine linen, more divine than the tent or blue sky, and the dipping in the dish.

(RF, 196)

312. (MacDonald recognized the ecological problems of the misuse of material things.)

The day would reveal a river stained with loathsome refuse, and rich gardens on hillsides mantled in sooty smoke and evil-smelling vapours sent up from a valley where men, like gnomes, toiled and caused to toil too eagerly. What would one think of a housekeeper so intent upon saving that she could waste no time on beauty or cleanliness? How many who would storm if they came home to an untidy house, feel no uneasiness that they have all day been defiling the house of the Father, nor at night lifted hand to cleanse it! Such men regard him as a fool whose joy a foul river can poison; yet as soon as they have by pollution gathered and saved their god, they make haste to depart from the spot they have ruined! Oh for an invasion of indignant ghosts, to drive from the old places the generation that dishonours the ancient Earth! The sun shows all their disfiguring, but the friendly night comes at length to hide her disgrace; and that well hidden, slowly ascends the brooding moon to conveil her beauty.

(HA, 13–14)

313. Which is more the possessor of the world—he who has a thousand houses, or he who, without one house to call his own, has ten in which his knock at the door would rouse instant jubilation? Which is the richer—the man who, his large money spent, would have no refuge; or he for whose necessity a hundred would sacrifice comfort? Which of the two possessed the earth—king Agrippa or tent-maker Paul?

(HG, 93)

314. Which is the real possessor of a book—the man who has its original and every following edition, and shows, to many an admiring and envying visitor, now this, now that, in binding characteristic, with possessor-pride ... or the man who cherishes one little, hollow-backed, coverless, untitled, bethumbed copy, which he takes with him in his solitary walks and broods over in his silent chamber,

always finding in it some beauty or excellence or aid he had not found before—which is to him in truth as a live companion?

(HG, 93–94)

315. When I trouble myself over a trifle, even a trifle confessed—the loss of some little article, say—spurring my memory, and hunting the house, not from immediate need, but from dislike of loss; when a book has been borrowed of me and not returned, and I have forgotten the borrower, and fret over the missing volume, while there are thousands on my shelves from which the moments thus lost might gather treasure holding relation with neither moth, nor rust, nor thief; am I not like the disciples? Am I not a fool whenever loss troubles me more than recovery would gladden? God would have me wise, and smile at the trifle. Is it not time I lost a few things when I care for them so unreasonably? This losing of things is of the mercy of God; it comes to teach us to let them go.

(SII, 53–54)

316. (Comments on Jesus' command to the rich young ruler to sell all he had.)

There was nothing like this in the law: was it not hard?—Hard to let earth go, and take heaven instead? For eternal life, to let dead things drop? To turn his back on Mammon, and follow Jesus? Lose his rich friends, and be of the Master's household? Let him say it was hard who does not know the Lord, who has never thirsted after righteousness, never longed for the life eternal!

(SII, 13)

317. There are good people who can hardly believe that, if the young man had consented to give up his wealth, the Lord would not then have told him to keep it; they too seem to think the treasure in heaven insufficient as a substitute. They cannot believe he would have been better off without his wealth. "Is not wealth power?" they ask. It is

indeed power, and so is a wolf hid in the robe; it is power, but as of a brute machine, of which the owner ill knows the handles and cranks, valves and governor. The multitude of those who read the tale are of the same mind as the youth himself—in his worse moment, as he turned and went—with one vast difference, that they are not sorrowful.

(SII, 35–36)

318. Because of possession the young man had not a suspicion of the grandeur of the call with which Jesus honoured him. He thought he was hardly dealt with to be offered a patent of Heaven's nobility—he was so very rich! *Things* filled his heart; things blocked up his windows; things barricaded his door, so that the very God could not enter. His soul was not empty, swept, and garnished, but crowded with meanest idols, among which his spirit crept about upon its knees, wasting on them the gazes that belonged to his fellows and his Master.

(SII, 47)

319. It is imperative on us to get rid of the tyranny of *things.*

(SII, 37)

320. Why should the rich fare differently from other people in respect of the world to come? They do not perceive that the law is they *shall* fare like other people, whereas they want to fare as rich people.

(SII, 22)

321. But with God all things are possible: He can save even the rich!

(L, 207)

322. He . . . has always been rich, and accustomed to have his own way! I begin to think one punishment of making money in a wrong manner is to be prosperous in it!

(WM, 339)

323. It takes a good many disgraceful things to bring a rich man to outward disgrace.

(WM, 179)

324. It must be one of the punishments of riches that they make the sight of poverty so disagreeable! To luxury, poverty is a living reproach.

(WM, 353)

325. But it is not the rich man only who is under the dominion of things; they too are slaves who, having no money, are unhappy from the lack of it. . . .

(SII, 39)

326. . . . the rich man who held his *things* lightly, nor let them nestle in his heart; who was a channel and no cistern; who was ever and always forsaking his money—starts, in the new world, side by side with the man who accepted, not hated, his poverty. Each will say, "I am free!"

(SII, 52)

327. But if thou art poor, then look not on thy purse when it is empty. He who desires more than God wills him to have, is also a servant of mammon, for he trusts in what God has made, and not in God Himself. He who laments what God has taken from him, he is a servant of mammon. He who for care can not pray, is a servant of mammon.

(PF, 34)

328. We are rich or poor according to what we are, not what we have.

(DE, 199)

329. "And shouldn't the poor be pitied?" said Christina.
"Not except they need pity."
"Is it not pitiable to be poor?"

"By no means. It is pitiable to be wretched—and that I venture to suspect, the rich are oftener than the poor."

(WM, 87)

330. (A fairy godmother's statement about the value of poverty.)

"Yes," she went on, "you have got to thank me that you are so poor, Peter. I have seen to that, and it has done well for both you and me, my friend. Things come to the poor that can't get in at the door of the rich. Their money somehow blocks it up. It is a great privilege to be poor, Peter—one that no man ever coveted, and but a very few have sought to retain, but one that yet many have learned to prize. You must not mistake, however, and imagine it a virtue; it is but a privilege, and one also that, like other privileges, may be terribly misused."

(PC, 51)

331. It is a hard thing for a rich man to grow poor; but it is an awful thing for him to grow dishonest, and some kinds of speculation lead a man deep into dishonesty before he thinks what he is about. Poverty will not make a man worthless—he may be worth a great deal more when he is poor than he was when he was rich; but dishonesty goes very far indeed to make a man of no value—a thing to be thrown out in the dust-hole of the creation, like a bit of a broken basin, or a dirty rag.

(AB, 139)

332. "... the rich withdraw themselves from the poor. Instead, for instance, of helping them to bear their burdens, they leave the still struggling poor of whole parishes to sink into hopeless want, under the weight of those who have already sunk beyond recovery. I am not sure that to shoot them would not involve less injustice. At all events he that hates his brother is a murderer."

"But there is no question of hating here," objected Mr. Marley.

"I am not certain that absolute indifference to one's neighbors is not as bad. It came to nearly the same thing in the case of the priest and the Levite, who passed by on the other side," said Mr. Blackstone.

(V, 167–68)

333. If the people who want to do good among the poor would give up patronizing them; would cease from trying to convert them before they have gained the smallest personal influence with them; would visit them as those who have just as good a right to be here as they have, it would be all the better for both, perhaps chiefly for themselves.

(RF, 205)

334. The part of philanthropist is indeed a dangerous one; and the man who would do his neighbour good must first study how not to do him evil and must begin by pulling the beam out of his own eye.

(L, 71)

335. Now Clementine was a radical of her day, a reformer, a leveller—one who complained bitterly that some should be so rich, and some so poor. In this she was perfectly honest. Her own wealth, from a vague sense of unrighteousness in the possession of it, was such a burden to her, that she threw it away where often it made other people stumble, if not fall.

(ML, 194–95)

336. He had a great respect for money, and much overrated its value as a means of doing even what *he* called good: religious people generally do—with a most unChristian dullness. We are not told that the Master made the smallest use of money for His end.

(SG, 278)

337. (The novel's heroine considers what to do with her life, which leads to comments by the author.)
She must not waste her life! She must *do* something!

What should it be? Her deep sense of the misery around her had of course suggested that it must be something in the way of help. But what form was the help to take? "I have not money!" she said to herself—for this, the last and feeblest of means for the doing of good, is always the first to suggest itself to one who has not perceived the mind of God in the matter. To me it seems that the first thing in regard to money is to prevent it from doing harm. The man who sets out to do good with his fortune is like one who would drive a team of tigers through the streets of a city, or hunt the fox with cheetahs. I would think of money as Christ thought of it, not otherwise; for no other way is true, however it may recommend itself to good men; and neither Christ nor His apostles did anything by means of money; nay, he who would join them in their labors had to abandon his fortune.

(WW, 46–47)

338. (Mr. Drake has just received a large inheritance.)

"Now, Mr. Wingfold, tell me plainly what you think the first thing I ought to do with this money toward making it a true gift of God. I mean what can I do with it for somebody else.... What do you count the first thing I should try to set right?"

"I should say *injustice*. My very soul revolts against the talk about kindness to the poor, when such a great part of their misery comes from the injustice and greed of the rich.... But even [Jesus] did not attack individuals to *make* them do right; and if you employ your money in doing justice to the oppressed and afflicted, to those shorn of the commonest rights of humanity, it will be the most powerful influence of all to wake the sleeping justice in the dull hearts of other men. It is the business of anybody who can, to set right what anybody has set wrong."

(At this point Mr. Wingfold gives a specific instance of an unjust landlord. Mr. Drake is able to buy out the land-lord and begin to treat the tenants justly.)

(PF, 185–86)

339. (Mr. Drake's work for flood protection for the poor has caused some inconvenience and slight expense for the rich.)

Their personal inconveniences were like the shifting cloud that hides the moon, and in the resentment they occasioned, blinded their hearts to the seriousness of the evils from which their merely temporary annoyance was the deliverance of their neighbors. A fancy of prescriptive right in their own comforts outweighed all the long and heavy sufferings of the others. Why should not their neighbors continue miserable, when they had been miserable all their lives hitherto? Those who on the contrary, had been comfortable all their lives, and liked it so much, ought to continue comfortable—even at their expense. Why not let well alone? Or if people would be so unreasonable as to want to be comfortable too, when nobody cared a straw about them, let them make themselves comfortable without annoying those superior beings who had been comfortable all the time! Persons who, consciously or unconsciously, reason thus, would do well to read with a little attention the parable of the rich man and Lazarus, wherein it seems recognized that a man's having been used to a thing may be just the reason, not for the continuance, but for the alteration of his condition.

(PF, 304–5)

340. Thus Jones the butcher—a man who never sold bad meat, never charged for an ounce more than he delivered, and when he sold to the poor, considered them. In buying and selling he had a weakness for giving the fair play he demanded. He had a little spare money somewhere, but he did not make a fortune out of hunger, retire early, and build churches. A local preacher once asked him if he knew what was the plan of salvation. He answered with the utmost innocence, cutting off a great lump of leg of beef for a family he had just told him was starving, that he hadn't an idea, but no Christian could doubt it was all right.

(PF, 125–26)

341. Mr. Drew! your shop is the temple of your service where the Lord Christ . . . is or ought to be, throned; your counter is, or ought to be, His altar; and everything thereon laid, with the intent of doing as well as you can for your neighbor, in the name of *the* Man Christ Jesus, is a true sacrifice offered to Him a service done to the eternal creating Love of the universe. . . . I say not," Polwarth went on, "that by so doing you will grow a rich man, but I say that by so doing you will be saved from growing too rich, and that you will be a fellow-worker with God for the salvation of His world."

"I must live; I cannot give my goods away!" murmured Mr. Drew. . . .

"That would be to go against the order of His world," said Polwarth. "No; a harder task is yours, Mr. Drew—to make your business a gain to you, and at the same time to be not only what is commonly counted just, but interested in, and careful of, and caring for your neighbor, as a servant of the God of bounty who giveth to all men liberally. Your calling is to do your best for your neighbor that you reasonably can."

"But who is to fix what is reasonable?" asked Drew.

"The man himself, thinking in the presence of Jesus Christ. There is a holy moderation which is of God."

"There won't be many fortunes—great fortunes— made after that rule, Mr. Polwarth."

"Very few."

"Then do you say that no great fortunes have been righteously made?"

"If *righteously* means *after the fashion of Jesus Christ*— But I will not judge: that is for the God-enlightened conscience of the man himself to do, not for his neighbor's. Why should I be judged by another man's conscience? But you see, Mr. Drew—and this is what I was driving at—you have it in your power to *serve* God through the needs of His children all the working day, from morning to night, so long as there is a customer in your shop."

(TW, 293–94)

342. (As a result of his mother's desertion, Shargar has no means of support. His schoolmates help him for a while.)

The friendship of Robert had gained Shargar the favorable notice of others of the school-public ... when his desertion was known, moved both by their compassion for him and their respect for Robert, they began to give him some portion of the dinner they brought with them; and never in his life had Shargar fared so well as for the first week after he had been cast upon the world. But in proportion as their interest faded with the novelty; so their appetites reasserted former claims and use and wont, and Shargar began once more to feel the pangs of hunger.

(RF, 56)

343. Mammon, the most contemptible of deities, is the most worshipped, both outside and in the house of God: to many of the religious rich, ... the great damning revelation will be their behaviour to the poor to whom they thought themselves very kind.

(SIII, 240)

344. "See how, even in the services of the church, as they call them, they will accumulate gorgeousness and cost. Had I my way, ... I would never have any vessel used in the eucharist but wooden platters and wooden cups."

"But are we not to serve Him with our best?" said my wife.

"Yes, with our very hearts and souls, with our absolute being. But all external things should be in harmony with the spirit of His revelation. And if God chose that His Son should visit the earth in homely fashion, in homely fashion likewise should be everything that enforces and commemorates that revelation. All church-form should be on the other side from show and expense. Let the money go to build decent houses for God's poor, not to give them His holy bread and wine out of silver and gold and precious stones—stealing from the significance of the content by the meretricious grandeur of the [container]. I would send all the church-plate to fight the devil with his own weapons in our overcrowded cities, and in our villages where the husbandmen are housed like swine, by giving them room to be clean, and decent air from heaven to breathe. When the people find the clergy thus in earnest, they will follow them fast enough, and the money will come in like salt and oil upon the sacrifice."

(SP, 51–52)

345. ... money is not mammon; it is God's invention; it is good and the gift of God. But for money and the need of it, there would not be half the friendship in the world. It is powerful for good when divinely used. Give it plenty of air, and it is sweet as the hawthorn; shut it up, and it cankers and breeds worms. Like all the best gifts of God, like the air and the water, it must have motion and change and shakings asunder; like the earth itself, like the heart and mind of man, it must be broken and turned, not heaped together and neglected. It is an angel of mercy, whose wings are full of balm and dews and refreshings; but when you lay hold of him, pluck his pinions, pen him in a yard, and fall down and worship him—then, with the blessed vengeance of his master, he deals plague and confusion and terror, to stay the idolatry.

(PF, 32)

346. How would you not spend your money for the Lord, if He needed it at your hand! He does need it; for he that spends it upon the least of his fellows, spends it upon his Lord. To hold fast upon God with one hand, and open wide the other to your neighbor—that is religion; that is the law and the prophets, and the true way to all better things that are yet to come.—Lord, defend us from Mammon. Hold Thy temple against his foul invasion. Purify our money with Thy air, and Thy sun, that it may be our slave, and Thou our Master. Amen.

(PF, 35)

347. (The remainder of this section is taken from the novel *Robert Falconer* and gives glimpses of Falconer's work among the poor of London. As a result of reading this novel, many young people committed their lives to working in London's slums. By sharing his own sorrows and the motivations for the work he is doing, Falconer convinced a poor unbeliever to help him with his personal labors among the poor of London.)

Before they parted, the unaccustomed tears had visited the eyes of DeFleuri, and he consented not only to repair Mrs. Chisolm's garret-floor, but to take in hand the expenditure of a certain sum weekly, as he should judge expedient, for the people who lived in that and the neighboring houses—in no case, however, except of sickness, or actual want of bread from want of work. Thus did Falconer appoint a sorrow-made infidel to be the almoner of his Christian charity, knowing well that the nature of the Son of Man was in him, and that to get him to do as the Son of Man did, in ever so small a degree, was the readiest means of bringing his higher nature to the birth.

(RF, 411)

348. (Lady Georgina, a very rich lady, offers to help Falconer in his "efforts for the elevation of the lower classes.")

I don't make any such efforts . . . I have only relations with individuals, none with classes.

(RF, 447)

349. The chief good which societies might effect would be the procuring of simple justice for the poor. That is what they need at the hands of the nation, and what they do not receive. . . . many could do something, if they would only set about it simply, and not be too anxious to convert them; if they would only be their friends after a common-sense fashion.

(RF, 450)

350. (Lady Georgina is obviously unfitted to work with the poor at this point in her life. At first she believes that she

only would need to dress differently, which leads to the
following remarks. This is only part of a lengthy conversation between Falconer and the lady. In spite of, or more
likely because of, the strong statements made by Falconer,
she eventually does participate in the help given to poor
people by the "little company.")

    ... No, Lady Georgina, it was not of a dress so easily
altered that I was thinking; it was of the *habit,* the dress of
mind, of thought, of feeling. When you laid aside your beautiful dress, could you avoid putting on the garment of *condescension,* the most unchristian virtue attributed to deity
or saint? ... —could your temper endure the mortifications
of low opposition and misrepresentation of motive ...
Could you be rudely, impudently, thwarted by the very persons for whom you were spending your strength and
means, and show no resentment? Could you make allow-
ances for them for your own brothers and sisters, your own
children? ... Could you endure the ugliness both moral and
physical which you must meet at every turn? Could you
look upon loathsomeness, not merely without turning away
in disgust, and thus wounding the very heart you would
heal, but without losing your belief in the Fatherhood of
God, by losing your faith in the actual blood-relationship to
yourself of these wretched beings?

    Would you not be tempted, for the sake of your own
comfort, if not for the pride of your own humanity, to believe that, like untimely blossoms, these must fall from off
the boughs of the tree of life, and come to nothing at all?—
a theory that may do for the preacher, but will not do for
the worker; him it would paralyze;—or, still worse, infinitely
worse, that they were doomed, from their birth, to endless
ages of a damnation, filthy as that in which you now found
them, and must probably leave them? If you could come to
this, you had better withhold your hand; for no desire for
the betterment of the masses, as they are stupidly called,
can make up for a lack of faith in the individual. If you
cannot hope for them in your heart, your hands cannot

reach them to do them good. They will only hurt them . . .
(RF, 448–49)

351. "And then the time you must spend before you can lay
hold upon [the poor] at all, that is with the personal relation which alone is of any real influence! Our Saviour Himself had to be thirty years in the world before He had footing enough in it to justify Him in beginning to teach
publicly; He had been laying the needful foundations all the
time. Not under any circumstances could I consent to make
use of you before you had brought yourself into genuine
relations with some of them first . . .
(RF, 449)

352. What I want is first to be their friend, and then to be at
length recognized as such. It is only in rare cases that I
seek the acquaintance of any of them; I let it come
naturally. I bide my time. Almost never, do I offer assistance. I wait till they ask for it, and then often refuse the
sort they want. The worst thing you can do for them is to
attempt to save them from the natural consequences of
wrong; you may sometimes help them out of them. But it is
right to do many things for them when you know them,
which it would not be right to do for them until you know
them. I am amongst them; they know me; their children
know me; and something is always occurring that makes
this or that one come to me. Once I have a footing, I seldom
lose it. So you see, in this my labor I am content to do the
thing that lies next me. I wait events.
(RF, 450–51)

353. [Falconer] knew that misery and wretchedness are the
right and best condition of those who live so that misery
and wretchedness are the natural consequences of their
life. But there ought always to be the possibility of emerg-
ing from these; and as things were, over the whole country,
for many who would if they could, it was impossible to
breathe the fresh air, to be clean, to live like human beings,

and he saw this difficulty ever on the increase, through the
capacity of the holders of small house-property, and the
utter wickedness of railway companies, who pulled down
every house that stood in their way, and did nothing to
provide room for those who were thus ejected—most probably from a wretched place, but only to be driven into a
more wretched still. To provide suitable dwellings for the
poor he considered the most pressing of all necessary re-
forms. His own fortune was not sufficient for doing much in
this way, but he set about doing what he could by purchas-
ing houses in which the poor lived, and putting them into
the hands of persons whom he could trust, and who were
immediately responsible to him for their proceedings; they
had to make them fit for human abodes, and let them to
those who desired better accommodation, giving the preference to those already tenants, as long as they paid their
reasonable rent, which he considered far more necessary
for them to do than for him to have done.

(RF, 454–55)

354. By degrees, without any laws or regulations, a little
company was gathered ... of men and women, who aided
each other, and without once meeting as a whole, labored
not the less as one body in the work of the Lord, bound in
one by bonds that had nothing to do with cobweb commit-
tee meeting or public dinners, chairmen or wine-flushed
subscriptions. They worked like the leaven of which the
Lord spoke.

(RF, 456)

NINE

 SELF

355. . . . for God's sake, do not cling to your own poor will. It is not worth having. It is a poor, miserable, degrading thing to fall down and worship the inclination of your own heart, which may have come from any devil, or from any accident of your birth, or from the weather, or from anything. Take the will of God, eternal, pure, strong, living and true, the only good thing; take that, and Christ will be your brother.

(GW, 128–29)

356. To will, not from self, but with the Eternal, is to live.

(SIII, 11)

357. But we must note that, although the idea of the denial of self is an entire and absolute one, yet the thing has to be done *daily:* we must keep on denying.

(SII, 222)

358. No one knows what a poor creature he is but the man who makes it his business to be true. The only mistake

worse than thinking well of himself, is for a man to think God takes no interest in him.

(WM, 198)

359. Man thinks his consciousness is himself; whereas his life consisteth in the inbreathing of God, and the consciousness of the universe of truth. To have himself, to know himself, to enjoy himself, he calls life; whereas, if he would forget himself, tenfold would be his life in God and his neighbours.

(SI, 214–15)

360. By health I mean that simple regard to the truth, to the will of God, which will turn away a man's eyes from his own conditions, and leave God free to work His perfection in him—free, that is, of the interference of the man's self-consciousness and anxiety.

(EA, 192)

361. To find God in others is better than to grow *solely* in the discovery of Him in ourselves, if indeed the latter were possible.

(EA, 227)

362. Respect and graciousness from each to each is of the very essence of Christianity, independently of rank, or possession or relations ... the man who thinks of the homage due to him, and not of the homage owing by him, is essentially rude.

(WM, 54)

363. He had a good opinion of himself—on what grounds I do not know; but he was rich ... I doubt if there is any more certain soil for growing a good opinion of oneself. Certainly, the more you try to raise one by doing what is right and worth doing, the less you succeed.

(WM, 6)

364. No good ever comes of pride, for it is the meanest of mean things, and no one but he who is full of it thinks it grand.

(MM, 74–75)

365. The desire to be known of men is destructive to all true greatness; nor is there any honor worth calling honor but what comes from an unseen source. To be great is to seem small in the eyes of men.

(DG, 244)

366. Beauchamp was no great favourite even in his own set; for there is one kind of religion in which the more devoted a man is, the fewer proselytes he makes: the worship of himself.

(AF, 151)

367. Dignity is such a delicate thing!

(L, 121)

368. As soon as even service is done for the honour and not for the service-sake, the doer is that moment outside the kingdom.

(SI, 16)

369. When the man arises with a servant's heart and a ruler's brain, then is the summer of the Church's content.

(EA, 6)

370. In thinking lovingly about others, we think healthily about ourselves.

(MM, 495)

371. It is a fundamental necessity of the kingdom of heaven, impossible as it must seem to all outside it, that each shall count other better than himself; it is the natural condition of the man God made, in relation to the other men God has made. Man is made, not to contemplate himself, but to behold in others the Beauty of the Father. A man

who lives to meditate upon and worship himself, is in the
slime of hell.

(HA, 77)

372. It is only through live relation to others that any individuality crystallizes.

(WM, 233)

373. . . . even the poorest love is the enemy of selfishness unto
the death, for the one or the other must give up the ghost.

(WC, 312)

374. No sooner had he yielded his pride, than he felt it
possible to love the man—not for anything he was, but for
what he might and must be.

(WM, 190)

375. What a hell of horror, I thought, to wander alone, a
bare existence never going out of itself, never widening its
life in another life, but, bound with the cords of its poor
peculiarities, lying an eternal prisoner in the dungeon of its
own being!

(L, 83)

376. It is in ordering our own thoughts and our own actions, that we have first to stand up for the right; our business is not to protect ourselves from our neighbor's wrong,
but our neighbor from our wrong. This is to slay evil; the
other is to make it multiply. A man who would pull out
even a mote from his brother's eye, must first pull out the
beam from his own eye, must be righteous against his own
selfishness. That is the only way to wound the root of evil.
He who teaches his neighbor to insist on his rights, is not a
teacher of righteousness. He who, by fulfilling his own duties, teaches his neighbor to give every man the fair play he
owes him, is a fellow-worker with God.

(WM, 349)

377. It is a good thing to desire to share a good thing, but it is not well to be unable alone to enjoy a good thing. It is our enjoyment that should make us desirous to share. What is there to share if the thing be of no value in itself? To enjoy alone is to be able to share.... It is not love alone but pride also, and often only pride, that leads to the desire for another to be present with us in possession.

(WM, 11–12)

378. But to try to make others comfortable is the only way to get right comfortable ourselves, and that comes partly of not being able to think so much about ourselves when we are helping other people. For our Selves will always do pretty well if we don't pay them too much attention. Our Selves are like some little children who will be happy enough so long as they are left to their own games, but when we begin to interfere with them and make them presents of too nice playthings, or too many sweet things, they begin at once to fret and spoil.

(AB, 167)

379. You see when he forgot his Self his mother took care of his Self, and loved and praised his Self. Our own praises poison our Selves, and puff and swell them up, till they lose all shape and beauty, and become like great toadstools. But the praises of father or mother do our Selves good, and comfort them and make them beautiful. *They* never do them any harm. If they do any harm, it comes of our mixing some of our own praises with them, and that turns them nasty and slimy and poisonous.

(AB, 167–68)

380. His own principles were existent only in a latent condition, undeveloped from good impulses and kind sentiments. For instance: he would help anyone whose necessity happened to make an impression upon him, but he never took pains to enter into the feelings of others—to under-

stand them from their own point of view: he never had said
to himself, "That is another me."

(AF, 216)

381. When self is first it simply makes devils of us.

(DG, 668)

382. I suspect that self-examination is seldom the most profitable, certainly it is sometimes the most unpleasant, and
always the most difficult of moral actions—that is, to perform
after a genuine fashion. I know that very little of what passes
for it has the remotest claim to reality; and I will not say it
has never to be done; but I am certain that a good deal of
energy spent by some devout and upright people on trying to
understand themselves and their own motives, would be ex-
pended to better purpose, and with far fuller attainment even
in regard to that object itself, in the endeavour to understand
God, and what He would have us do.

(ML, 196)

383. "You must follow the truth, and, in that pursuit, the
less one thinks about himself, the pursuer, the better." Let
him so hunger and thirst after the truth that the vision of it
occupies all his being, and leaves no time to think of his
hunger and his thirst. Self-forgetfulness in the reaching out
after that which is essential to us is the healthiest of mental
conditions. One has to look to his way, to his deeds, to his
conduct—not to himself. In such losing of the false, or
merely reflected, we find the true self. There is no harm in
being stupid, so long as a man does not think himself clever; no good in being clever, if a man thinks himself so, for
that is a short way to the worst stupidity. If you think
yourself clever, set yourself to do something; then you will
have a chance of humiliation.

(MM, 45)

384. . . . our feelings, especially where a wretched self is
concerned, are notably illogical.

(PF, 136)

385. The Self, when it finds it cannot have honour because of its gifts, because of the love lavished upon it, because of its conquests, and the "golden opinions bought from all sorts of people," will please itself with the thought of its abnegations, of its unselfishness, of its devotion to God, of its forsakings for His sake. It may not *call* itself, but it will soon *feel* itself a saint, a superior creature, looking down upon the foolish world and its ways, walking on high "above the smoke and stir of this dim spot";—all the time dreaming a dream of utter folly, worshipping itself with the more concentration that it has yielded the approbation of the world, and dismissed the regard of others: even they are no longer necessary to its assurance of its own worths and merits! In a thousand ways will Self delude itself, in a thousand ways befool its own slavish being.

(SII, 220–21)

386. (A wife's love and delight in her husband may seem like pride but is not.)

It was with something very like pride, yet surely nothing evil, that she would watch the quick blows of his brawny arm as he beat the cold iron on the anvil till it was all aglow like the sun that lighted the world—then struck it into the middle of his coals, and blew softly with his bellows till the flame on the altar of his work-offering was awake and keen.

(MM, 459)

387. (How pride kept a father from loving his children.)

There was a great deal of self-satisfaction mixed up with the man's honesty, and the sooner that had a blow the better—it might prove a death-blow in the long run. It was pride that lay at the root of his hardness. . . . His daughter had disgraced him; and he was ready to flash into wrath with his son upon any imputation which recalled to him the torture he had undergone when his daughter's disgrace came first to the light. Her he had never forgiven, and now his pride flung his son out after her upon the first suspicion. . . . His pride paralysed his love. He thought more about himself than about his children. His own shame out-weighed in his estimation the sadness of their guilt. It was a less matter that they shoud be guilty, than that he, their father, should be disgraced.

(AN, 266)

388. . . . the faith of Jesus in His God and Father is, even now, setting me free from my one horror, selfishness; making my life an unspeakable boon to me, letting me know its roots in the eternal and perfect; giving me such love to my fellow, that I trust at last to love Him as Christ has loved me.

(PF, 211–12)

389. . . . the one principle of hell is—"I am my own. I am my own king and my own subject. *I* am the centre from which go out my thoughts; *I* am the object and end of my thoughts; back upon *me* as the alpha and omega of life, my thoughts return. My own glory is, and ought to be, my chief care; my ambition, to gather the regards of men to the one centre, myself."

(SIII, 102)

390. Perhaps his only vice was self-satisfaction—which few will admit to be a vice; remonstrance never reached him; to himself he was ever in the right, judging himself only by his sentiments and vague intents, never by his actions; that these had little correspondence never struck him; it had never even struck him that they ought to correspond.

(MM, 51)

391. Like most men, he was so well satisfied with himself that he saw no occasion to take trouble to be anything better than he was. Never suspecting what a noble creature he was meant to be, he never saw what a poor creature he was.

(MM, 157)

392. A repentant sinner feels that he is making himself little when he prays to be made humble: the Christian philosopher sees such a glory and spiritual wealth in humility that it appears to him almost too much to pray for.

(EA, 231–32)

393. (Following are some comments about a certain class of hymns.)

What pleased me in them was their full utterance of personal devotion to the Saviour, and ... what displeased me was a sort of sentimental regard of self in the matter—an implied special, and thus partially exclusive predilection or preference of the Saviour for the individual supposed to be making use of them; a certain fundamental want of humility therefore, although the forms of speech in which they were cast might be laboriously humble.

(V, 314)

394. No man's dignity is affected by what another does to him, but only by what he does, or would like to do, himself.

(MM, 222)

395. He ceased thinking, gave way to the feeling that God dealt hardly with him, and sat stupidly indulging a sense of grievance—with self-pity, than which there is scarce one more childish or enfeebling in the whole circle of the emotions.

(PF, 53)

396. That which is within a man, not that which lies beyond his vision, is the main factor in what is about to befall him. . . .

(L, 81)

397. I learned that it is better, a thousand-fold, for a proud man to fall and be humbled, than to hold up his head in his pride and fancied innocence. I learned that he that will be a hero, will barely be a man; that he that will be nothing but a

doer of his work, is sure of his manhood.

(PH, 166)

398. I think humiliation is a very different condition of mind from humility. Humiliation no man can desire: it is shame and torture. Humility is the true right condition of humanity—peaceful, divine. And yet a man may gladly welcome humiliation when it comes, if he finds that with a fierce shock and rude revulsion it has turned him right round, with his face away from pride, whither he was traveling and towards humility, however far away upon the horizon's verge she may sit waiting for him.

(AN, 273–74)

399. But indeed the business of the universe is to make such a fool of you that you will know yourself for one, and so begin to be wise!

(L, 26)

400. For to be ashamed is a holy and blessed thing. Shame is a thing to shame only those who want to appear, not those who want to be. . . . For to be humbly ashamed is to be plunged in the cleansing bath of the truth.

(SIII, 238)

401. She had so long practiced the art of deceiving herself that she was skillful at it. Indeed, but for the fault she had committed, she would all her life long have been given to petting and pitying, justifying and approving of herself. One can not help sometimes feeling that the only chance for certain persons is to commit some fault sufficient to shame them out of the self-satisfaction in which they burrow. A fault, if only it be great and plain enough to exceed their powers of self-justification, may then be, of God's mercy, not indeed an angel of light to draw them, but verily a goblin of darkness to terrify them out of themselves. For the powers of darkness are His servants also.

(PF, 289)

402. His pride was bitterly wounded. Would it had been mortally! But pride seems in some natures to thrive upon wounds, as in others does love.

(PF, 265)

403. His pride was as strong as ever, and both helped him get over his suffering, and prevented him from getting the good of it.

(MM, 392)

404. (A man's meditation after some bitter experiences.)
    What is called a man's love for himself, is not love; it is but a phantastic resemblance of love . . . A man cannot love himself. . . . I sickened at the site of myself: how could I ever get rid of the demon? The same instant I saw the one escape: I must offer it back to its source—commit it to the One who had made it. I must live no more from it, but from the source of it; seek to know nothing more of it than he gave me to know by his presence therein. . . . What flashes of self-consciousness might cross me, should be God's gift, not of my seeking, and offered again to Him in ever new self-sacrifice. Alas! Alas! This I saw then, and this I yet see; but oh, how far am I still from that divine annihilation! The only comfort is, God is, and I am His, else I should not be at all.

(WC, 416–17)

405. (A young minister's thoughts on the danger of pride.)
    "One thing I dare to hope—that at the first temptation to show-off, I shall be made aware of my danger, and have the grace given me to pull up. . . . I know I shall make many blunders and do the things very badly; but failure itself will help to save me from conceit—will keep me, I hope, from thinking of myself at all, enabling me to leave myself in God's hands, willing to fail if He please."

(SF, 310)

406. Knowing herself a nobody, she now first began to be a somebody.

(ML, 368)

407. In the human being humility and greatness are not only correlative, but are one and the same condition.

(WW, 267)

408. He [a meek person] can imagine no bliss, no good in being greater than some one else. He is unable to wish himself other than he is, except more what God made him for, which is indeed the highest willing of the will of God.

(HG, 87)

409. We cannot see the world as God means it, save in proportion as our souls are meek. . . . Meekness alone makes the spiritual retina pure to receive God's things as they are, mingling with them neither imperfection nor impurity of its own.

(HG, 91)

410. It is enough that the man who refuses to assert himself, seeking no recognition by men, leaving the care of his life to the Father, and occupying himself with the will of the Father, shall find himself, by and by, at home in the Father's house, with all the Father's property his.

(HG, 93)

411. . . . whoever loves and cares for his appearance before the eyes of men, finds himself accused [in his own mind] of paltry follies, stupidities, and indiscretions, and punished with paltry mortifications, chagrins, and anxieties. From such arraignment no man is free, but him who walks in the perfect law of liberty—that is, the will of the Perfect—which alone is peace.

(ML, 47)

412. Self-will is weakness; the will to do the right is strength; Molly willed the right thing and held to it. Hence it was that she was so gentle. She walked lightly over the carpet, because she could run up a hill like a hare. When she caught selfishness in her, she was down upon it with the knee and grasp of a giant. Strong is the man or woman whose eternal life subjects the individual liking to the perfect will. Such man, such woman, is free man, free woman.

(HA, 275–76)

413. (Humility brings freedom to a pastor performing an unwelcome duty.)

Wingfold approached her with the air of a man who knew himself unwelcome but did not much mind—for he had not to care about himself.

(TB, 165)

414. Even in our nurseries, a joyful child is rarely selfish, generally righteous. It is not selfish to be joyful. What power could prevent him who sees the face of God from being joyful?—that bliss is his which lies behind all other bliss, without which no other bliss could ripen or last. The one bliss of the universe is the presence of God....

(SII, 227)

415. There is no joy belonging to human nature, as God made it, that shall not be enhanced a hundredfold to the man who gives up himself—though, in so doing, he may seem to be yielding the very essence of life.

(SII, 225)

 LOVE

416. Our Lord Himself taught a divine morality, which is as it were the body of love, and is as different from *mere* morality as the living body is from the dead.

(EA, 60)

417. Is power or love the making might of the universe? He who answers this question aright possesses the key to all righteous questions.

(EA, 79)

418. ... love, not hate, is deepest in what Love "loved into being."

(L, 94)

419. "He never said, 'You must all think the same way!' But He did say 'You must all love one another, and not fight!' "
(SF*, 5)

---

*Indicates translation of Scottish dialect into English.

420. Opinion is often the very death of love. Love aright, and you will come to think aright; and those who think aright must think the same. In the meantime, it matters nothing. The thing that does matter is that whereto we have attained, by that we should walk.

(DO, 293)

421. Surely then inasmuch as man is made in the image of God, nothing less than a love in the image of God's love, all-embracing, quietly excusing, heartily commending, can constitute the blessedness of man; a love not insensible to that which is foreign to it, but overcoming it with good.

(DO, 213–14)

422. But as the love of Him who is love, transcends ours as the heavens are higher than the earth, so must He desire in His child infinitely more than the most jealous love of the best mother can desire in hers. He would have him rid of all discontent, all fear, all grudging, all bitterness in word or thought, all gauging and measuring of his own with a different rod from that he would apply to another's. He will have no curling of the lip; no indifference in him to the man whose service in any form he uses; no desire to excell another, no contentment at gaining by his loss. He will not have him receive the smallest service without gratitude; would not hear from him a tone to jar the heart of another, a word to make it ache, be the ache ever so transient.

(HG, 12)

423. I want to help you to grow as beautiful as God meant you to be when He thought of you first.

(ML, 80)

424. Love has ever in view the absolute loveliness of that which it beholds. Where loveliness is incomplete, and love cannot love its fill of loving, it spends itself to make more lovely, that it may love more. . . .

(SI, 27)

425. For a man may see visions manifold, and believe them all; and yet his faith shall not save him; something more is needed—he must have that presence of God in his soul, of which the Son of Man spoke, saying: "If a man love Me, he will keep My words; and My Father will love him, and We will come unto him, and make Our abode with him." God in him he will be able to love for very love's sake; God not in him his best love will die into selfishness.

(WC, 419)

426. The law comes to make us long for the needful grace,—that is, for the divine condition, in which love is all, for God is Love.

(SI, 193)

427. . . . . the first words which follow for the setting forth of that grace whereby we may serve God acceptably are these—"Let brotherly love continue." To love our brother is to worship the Consuming Fire.

(SI, 32)

428. For love is divine, and then most divine when it loves according to *needs* and not according to *merits*.

(SI, 79)

429. Love without religion is the plucked rose. Religion without love—there is no such thing. Religion is the bush that bears all the roses; for religion is the natural condition of man in relation to the eternal facts, that is the truths, of his own being. To live is to love; there is no life but love. What shape the love puts on, depends on the persons between whom is the relation. The poorest love with religion, is better, because truer, therefore more lasting, more genuine, more endowed with the possibility of persistence—that is, of infinite development, than the most passionate devotion between man and woman without it.

(WM, 202–3)

430. I saw now that a man alone is but a being that may become a man—that he is but a need, and therefore a possibility.... A man to be perfect—complete, that is, in having reached the spiritual condition of persistent and universal growth, which is the mode wherein he inherits the infinitude of his Father—must have the education of a world of fellow-men.

(L, 102–3)

431. ... if I turned from every show of love lest it should be feigned, how was I ever to find the real love which must be somewhere in every world?

(L, 123)

432. The first thing a kindness deserves is acceptance, the next is transmission: Gibbie gave both, without thinking much about either.

(SG, 40)

433. Let no man who wants to do something for the soul of a man lose a chance of doing something for his body.

(SP, 238)

434. The man who thoroughly loves God and his neighbour is the only man who will love a woman ideally—who can love her with the love God thought of between them when he made man male and female. The man, I repeat, who loves God with his very life, and his neighbour as Christ loves him, is the man who alone is capable of grand, perfect, glorious love to any woman.

(SG, 416)

435. ... every man in love shows better than he is, though, thank God, not better than he is meant to become.

(AF, 271)

436. To save man or woman, the next thing to the love of God is the love of man or woman; only let no man or

woman mistake the love of love for love!

She started, grew white, stood straight up, grew red as a sunset:—was it—could it be?—"Is this love?" she said to herself, and for minutes she hardly moved.

It was love. Whether love was in her or not, she was in love—and it might get inside her.

(WM, 236)

437. Perhaps the best thing for the princess would have been to fall in love. . . . As for her own feelings on the subject, she did not even know that there was such a beehive of honey and stings to be fallen into.

(GK, 70)

438. Richard had not yet arrived at any readiness to fall in love. It is well when this readiness is delayed until the individuality is sufficiently developed to have its own demands. I venture to think one cause of unhappiness in marriages is, that each person's peculiar self was not, at the time of engagement, sufficiently grown for a natural selection of the suitable, that is, the *correspondent;* and that the development which follows is in most cases the development of what is reciprocally non-correspondent, and works for separation and not approximation. The only thing to overcome this or any other disjunctive power is development in the highest sense, that is, development of the highest and deepest in us—which can come only by doing right. The man who is growing to be one with his own nature, that is, one with God who is the *naturing* nature, is coming nearer and nearer to every one of his fellow-beings. This may seem a long way round to love, but it is the only road by which we can arrive at true love of any kind; and he who does not walk in it will one day find himself on the verge of a gulf of hate.

(TB, 105–6)

439. While one is yet only *in love,* the real person, the love capable, lies covered with the rose-leaves of a thousand

sleepy-eyed dreams, and through them come to the dreamer but the barest hints of the real person of whom is the dream. A thousand fancies fly out, approach, and cross, but never meet; the man and the woman are pleased, not with each other, but each with the fancied other. The merest common likings are taken for signs of a wonderful sympathy, of a radical unity—of essential capacity, therefore, of loving and being loved; at a hundred points their souls seem to touch, but their contacts are the merest brushings as of insect antennae; the real man, the real woman, is all the time asleep under the rose-leaves. Happy is the rare fate of the true—to wake and come forth and meet in the majesty of the truth, in the image of God, in their very being, in the power of that love which alone is being. They love, not this and that about each other, but each the very other—a love as essential to reality, to truth, to religion, as the love of the very God. Where such love is, let the difference of taste, the unfitnesses of temperament be what they may, the two must by and by be thoroughly one.

(WM, 201)

440. There are women who desire to be the *sole* object of a man's affection, and are all their lives devoured by unlawful jealousies.

(SG, 416)

441. They did not understand any human feeling—not even the silliness they called *love*—a godless, mindless affair, fit only for the doll-histories invented by children: they had a feeling, or a feeling had them, till another feeling came and took its place. When a feeling was there, they felt as if it would never go; when it was gone, they felt as if it had never been; when it returned, they felt as if it had never gone.

(WM, 117)

442. Was he in love with her? I do not know. I could tell, if I knew what being in love is. I think no two loves were ever

the same since the creation of the world. I know that something had passed from her eyes to his—but what? He may
have been in love with her already; but ere long my reader
may be more sure than I that he was not. The Maker of men
alone understands His awful mystery between the man and
woman. But without it, frightful indeed as are some of its
results, assuredly the world He has made would burst its
binding rings and fly asunder in shards, leaving His spirit
nothing to enter, no time to work His lovely will.

(PF, 27)

443. He thought about her till he fell asleep, and dreamed
about her till he woke. Not for a moment, however, did he
fancy he was in love with her; the feeling was different from
any he had hitherto recognized as embodying that passion.
It was the recognition and consequent admiration of a
beauty which every one who beheld it must recognize and
admire. . . .

(DE, 425)

444. . . . he grew more and more in love with Lucy. He almost loved her.

(GC, 68)

445. He loved as a man loves who has thought seriously,
speculated, tried to understand; whose love therefore is
consistent with itself, harmonious with its nature and history, changing only in form and growth, never in substance
and character. . . . The painter was not merely in love with
Florimel: he loved her.

(ML, 124)

446. And I said, "O Lord leave me not, for although I would
now in my turn right gladly die for her, yet would I not look
upon that woman again if the love of her would make me
love Thee one hair the less—Thou knowest." And the Lord
smiled upon me and said, "Fear not . . . My love infolds and
is the nest of all love". . . . And I arose and followed Him.

And every tree and flower, yea every stone and cloud, with the whole earth and sea and air, were full of God, even the living God—so that now I could have died of pure content. And I followed my Lord.

(TW, 498)

447. They were the happiest couple in that country, because they always understood each other, and that was because they always meant the same thing, and that was because they always loved what was fair and true and right better, not than anything else, but than everything else put together.

(PC, 36–37)

448. . . . the wife walked beside the husband in the strength of a faith in absolute Good. . . . She loved every hair upon his head, but loved his well-being infinitely more than his mortal life.

(PF, 30)

449. "What do you think the first duty of married people, Mercy—to each other I mean," he said.

"To be always what they look," answered Mercy.

"Yes, but I mean actively: what is it their first duty to do towards each other?"

"I can't answer that without thinking."

"Is it not each to help the other to do the will of God?"

"I would say yes, if I were sure I really meant it."

"You will mean it one day."

"Are you sure God will teach me?"

"I think He cares more to do that than anything else."

"More than to save us?"

"What is saving but taking us out of the dark into the light? There is no salvation but to know God and grow like Him."

(WM, 301)

450. The good for which we are born into this world is, that we may learn to love. . . . There are people—oh, such silly

people they are!—though they may sometimes be pleasing—who are always wanting people to love them. They think so much of themselves, that they want to think more; and to know that people love them makes them able to think more of themselves. They even think themselves loving because they are fond of being loved!

Such lovers are only selfish in a deeper way, and are more to blame than other selfish people; for, loving to be loved, they ought the better to know what an evil thing it is not to love; what a mean thing to accept what they are not willing to give. Even to love only those that love us, is, as the Lord has taught us, but a pinched and sneaking way of loving.

(RS, 71–72)

451. Gibbie's was love simple, unselfish, undemanding—not merely asking for no return, but asking for no recognition, requiring not even that its existence should be known. He was a rare one, who did not make the common miserable blunder of taking the shadow cast by love—the desire, namely, to be loved—for love itself.... Silly youths and maidens count themselves martyrs of love, when they are but the pining witnesses to a delicious and entrancing selfishness. But do not mistake me through confounding, on the other hand, the desire to be loved—which is neither wrong nor noble, any more than hunger is neither wrong or noble....

(SG, 415)

452. The sisters were about as good friends as such negative creatures could be; and they would be such friends all their lives, if on the one hand neither of them grew to anything better, and on the other no jealousy, or marked difference of social position through marriage, intervened. They loved each other, if not tenderly, yet with the genuineness of healthy family-habit—a thing not to be despised, for it keeps the door open for something better. In itself it is not at all to be reckoned upon, for habit is but the merest

shadow of reality. Still it is not a small thing, as families go, if sisters and brothers do not dislike each other.

(WM, 13–14)

453. They had enough of affection left for each other to preserve them from being absolutely cruel for cruelty's sake to those that came in their way....

(PG, 15)

454. You like me, because I am fortunate enough to please you—to be a gentleman, I hope—to be a man of some education, and capable of understanding, or at least docile enough to try to understand, what you tell me of your plans and pursuits. But you do not feel any relation to me on the ground of my humanity—that God made me, and therefore I am your brother. It is not because we grow out of the same stem, but merely because my leaf is a little like your own that you draw to me. Our Lord took on Him the nature of man: you will only regard your individual attractions. Disturb your liking and your love vanishes.

(AN, 384)

455. Mr. Fuller was a middle-aged man, who all his conscious years had been trying to get nearer to his brethren, moved thereto by the love he bore to the Father. The more anxious he was to come near to God, the more he felt that the high-road to God lay through the forest of humanity. And he had learned that love is not a feeling to be called up at will in the heart, but the reward as the result of an active exercise of the privileges of a neighbor.

(GC, 174)

456. The man who serves his fellow that he himself may be noble, misses the mark. He alone who follows the truth, not he who follows nobility, shall attain the noble. A man's nobility will, in the end, prove just commensurate with his humanity—with the love he bears his neighbor—not the amount of work he may have done for him. A man might

throw a lordly gift to his fellow, like a bone to a dog, and damn himself in the deed. You may insult a dog by the way you give him his bone.

(PF, 207)

457. I am certain that it is impossible to keep the law towards one's neighbour except one loves him.

(SI, 190)

458. A man must not choose his neighbour; he must take the neighbour that God sends him. In him, whoever he be, lies, hidden or revealed, a beautiful brother. The neighbour is just the man who is next to you at the moment, the man with whom any business has brought you in contact.

(SI, 210)

459. There was a time when I could not understand that he who loved not his brother was a murderer: now I see it to be no figure of speech, but, in the realities of man's moral and spiritual nature, an absolute simple fact. The murderer and the unloving sit on the same bench before the judge of eternal truth. The man who loves not his brother I do not say is at this moment capable of killing him, but if the natural working of his unlove be not checked, he will assuredly become capable of killing him. Until we love our brother—yes until we love our enemy, who is yet our brother—we contain within ourselves the undeveloped germ of murder.

(TW, 341)

460. Except I love my neighbour as myself, I may one day betray him! Let us therefore be compassionate and humble, and hope for every man.

(SIII, 242)

461. (A daughter asks her father if he thinks there is something of worth in every person and receives the following answer.)

Indeed I do; though I have met more than one in my lifetime concerning whom I felt compelled to say that it wanted keener eyes than mine, for there are more loving eyes. Myself I have been able to see good very clearly where some could see none; and shall I doubt that God can see good where my mole-eyes see none? Be sure of this that as He is keen-eyed for the evil in His creatures to destroy it, He would, if it were possible, be yet keener-eyed for the good to nourish and cherish it.

(V, 117)

462. "Would you feel bound to love a man because he was a fellowcountryman?"

"Other things being equal, I could not help it."

"Other things not being equal,—?"

"I should love the best man best. . . ."

"That is as I thought of you. For my part, my love for my own people has taught me to love every man, be his colour or country what it may. The man whose patriotism is not leading him in that direction has not yet begun to be a true patriot. Let him go to St. Paul and learn, or stay in his own cellar and be an idiot."

(WM, 243)

463. Is it then reasonable to love our enemies? God does; therefore it must be the highest reason. But is it reasonable to expect that man should become capable of doing so? Yes; on one ground: that the divine energy is at work in man, to render at length man's doing divine as his nature is. For this our Lord prayed when He said: "That they all may be one, as Thou, Father, art in Me, and I in Thee, that they also may be one in Us." Nothing could be less likely to human judgment: our Lord knows that one day it will come.

(SI, 218–19)

464. It may be an infinitely less evil to murder a man than to refuse to forgive him. The former may be the act of a moment of passion: the latter is the heart's choice. It is

spiritual murder, the worse, to hate, to brood over the feeling that excludes, that, in our microcosm, kills the image, the idea of the hated.

(SI, 83)

465. Now hate keeps its object present even more than the opposite passion. Love makes everything lovely; hate concentrates itself on the one thing hated.

(AF, 192)

466. ... we are as God made us.—No, I will not say that: I will say rather, I am as God is making me, and I shall one day be as He has made me. Meantime I know that He will have me love my enemy tenfold more than now I love my friend.

(PF, 29)

467. ... the grandest exercise of justice is mercy .... Confusion comes from the fancy that justice means *vengeance upon sin,* and not *the doing of what is right.* Justice can be at no strife with mercy, for not to do what is just would be most unmerciful.

(EA, 150)

468. No one can be just without love.

(ML, 170)

469. Love is the law of our condition, without which we can no more render justice than a man can keep a straight line walking in the dark.

(SI, 225)

470. Some things seem the harder to forgive the greater the love. It is but a false seeming, thank God, and comes only of selfishness, which makes both the love and the hurt seem greater than they are.

(WW, 531)

471. (Tibby, a blind woman, criticized Thomas frankly, but out of love.)

There was not a person in Glamerton who would have dared to speak thus to Thomas Crann but Tibby Dyster, perhaps because there was not one who had such a respect for him. Possibly the darkness about her made her bolder; but I think it was her truth, which is another word for *love,* however unlike love the outcome may look, that made her able to speak in this fasion.

(AF, 229)

472. And if he is severe, it is with the severity of love that will speak only the truth.

(SP, 284)

473. There are tender-hearted people who virtually object to the whole scheme of creation; they would neither have force used nor pain suffered; they talk as if kindness could do everything, even where it is not felt. Millions of human beings but for suffering would never develop an atom of affection. The man who would spare *due* suffering is not wise. It is folly to conclude a thing ought not to be done because it hurts. There are powers to be born, creations to be perfected, sinners to be redeemed, through the ministry of pain, that could be born, perfected, redeemed, in no other way.

(WM, 71–72)

474. Everything painful was to her cruel, and softness and indulgence, moral honey and sugar and nuts to all alike, was the panacea for human ills. She could not understand that infliction might be loving kindness. . . . She would have taken the whole world to her infinite heart, and in unwisdom coddled it into corruption. Praised be the grandeur of the God who can endure to make and see His children suffer. Thanks be to Him for His north winds and His poverty, and His bitterness that falls upon the spirit that errs: let

those who know Him, thus praise the Lord for His
goodness.

(ML, 158–59)

475. It is not good at all . . . to do everything for those you
love, and not give them a share in the doing. It's not kind.
It's making too much of yourself, my child.

(AB, 110–11)

476. A man must learn to love his children, not because they
are his, but because they are *children,* else his love will be
scarcely a better thing at last than the party-spirit of the
faithful politician. I doubt if it will prove even so good a thing.

(AF, 40)

477. . . . and the mother's heart more than any other God
has made is like Him in power of loving. Alas that she is so
seldom like Him in wisdom—so often thwarting the work of
God, and rendering more severe His measures with her
child by her attempts to shield him from His law, and save
him from saving sorrow.

(WW, 55)

478. You see, she loved you so much that she could think
of nothing or nobody but yourself! That is the way of mothers, Jamie, if you only knew it. She was close to sinning an
awful sin for your sake!

(SF*, 286)

479. It is the loveliest provision, doubtless, that every child
should have a mother of his own; but there is a mother-love
which I had almost called divine—the love, namely, that a
woman bears to a child because he is a child, regardless of
whether he be her own or another's. It is that they may

---

*Indicates translation of Scottish into English.

learn to love thus, that women have children. Some women love so without having any.

(RS, 51–52)

480. (Curdie and his mother each work hard to provide good things for the other one.)
Not that she and Curdie ever thought of how much they worked for each other: that would have spoiled everything.

(PG, 83–84)

481. I knew now, that it is by loving, and not by being loved, that one can come nearest the soul of another; yea, that, where two love, it is the loving of each other, and not the being beloved by each other, that originates and perfects and assures their blessedness.

(PH, 181)

482. . . . to understand is not more wonderful than to love.

(L, 57)

483. "There are things I cannot explain," she replied, "until you have become capable of understanding them—which can only be when love is grown perfect."

(L, 130)

484. Love is the true revealer of secrets, because it makes one with the object regarded.

(DO, 117)

485. To explain to him who loves not, is but to give him the more plentiful material for misinterpretation.

(TW, 347)

486. Intelligence is a consequence of love; nor is there any true intelligence without it.

(AN, 478)

 GOD'S LOVE

487. . . . for God is love, and Love is that which is, and was, and shall be for evermore—boundless, unconditioned, self-existent, creative! "Truly," he said to himself, "God is love, and God is all and in all! He is not abstraction; He is the one eternal Individual God! In Him love evermore breaks forth anew into fresh personality—in every new consciousness, in every new child of the one creating Father. In every burning heart, in everything that hopes and fears and is, Love is the creative presence, the centre, the course of life, yea Life itself; yea, God Himself!"

(SF, 166–67)

488. The love of God is the perfecting of every love.

(SIII, 195)

489. "But the Deity you talk of—"

"I beg your pardon, my lord: I talked of no deity; I talked of a living Love that gave us birth and calls us His children. Your deity I know nothing of."

(M, 429)

490. (A young couple, caught in a flash flood, are clinging to a stone wall.)

"I can't help being frightened!" she panted.

"We are in God's arms," returned Ian. "He is holding us."

"Are you sure we shall not be drowned?" she asked.

"No; but I am sure the water cannot take us out of God's arms."

(WM, 226)

491. I know that good is coming to me—that good is always coming; though few have at all times the simplicity and the courage to believe it. What we call evil, is the only and best shape, which, for the person and his condition at the time, could be assumed by the best good.

(PH, 185)

492. James Blatherwick was of such whose sluggish natures require, for the melting of their stubbornness, and their remoulding into forms of strength and beauty, such a concentration of the love of God that it becomes a consuming fire.

(SF, 226)

493. Therefore all that is not beautiful in the beloved, all that comes between and is not of love's kind, must be destroyed.

And our God is a consuming fire.

(SI, 28)

494. He gives Himself to us—shall not we give ourselves to Him? Shall we not give ourselves to each other whom He loves?

(SI, 21)

495. . . . God drew [him] ever more and more strongly; until at last—I know not, I say, how God did it, or whereby He made the soul of James Blatherwick different from what it

had been—but at last it grew capable of loving, and did love: first, he yielded to love because he could not help it; then he willed to love because he *could* love; then, become conscious of the power, he loved the more, and so went on to love more and more. And thus did James become what he had to become—or perish.

(SF, 252–53)

496. Until love, which is the truth towards God, is able to cast out fear, it is well that fear should hold; it is a bond, however poor, between that which is and that which creates—a bond that must be broken, but a bond that can be broken only by the tightening of an infinitely closer bond.

(SII, 159)

497. Although He loves them utterly, He does not tell them there is nothing in Him to make them afraid. That would be to drive them from Him for ever. While they are such as they are, there is much in Him that cannot but affright them; they ought, they do well to fear Him.

(SII, 160)

498. I remembered that God was near me. But I did not know what God is then as I know now, and when I thought about Him then, which was neither much nor often, my idea of Him was not like Him; it was merely a confused mixture of other people's fancies about Him and my own. I had been told that He was angry with those that did wrong; I had not understood that He loved them all the time, although He was displeased with them and must punish them to make them good.

(RB, 35–36)

499. Neither power nor wisdom, though infinite both, could constitute a God worthy of the worship of a human soul; and the worship of such a God must sink to the level of that fancied divinity.

(EA, 277)

500. Oh the summer days, with the hot sun drawing the odors from the feathery larches and the white-stemmed birches, when, getting out of the water, I would lie in the warm, soft grass, where now and then the tenderest little breeze would creep over my skin, until, the sun baking me more than was pleasant, I would rouse myself with an effort, and running down to the fringe of rushes that bordered the full-brimmed river, plunge again headlong into the quiet brown water and dabble and swim till I was once more weary. For innocent animal delights I know of nothing to match those days—so warm, yet so pure-aired—so clean, so glad. I often think how God must love His little children to have invented for them such delights! For of course, if He did not love the children and delight in their pleasure He would not have invented the two and brought them together. Yes, my child, I know what you would say: "How many there are who have no such pleasures!" I grant it sorrowfully, but you must remember that God has not done with them yet; and besides, that there are more pleasures in the world than you or I know anything about. And if we had it *all* pleasure, I know I should not care so much about what is better, and I would rather be good than have any other pleasure in the world, and so would you, though perhaps you do not know it yet.

(RB, 113–14)

501. (The children referred to in the following include all humans, children of God, not just those who are young.)

All sorts of means are kept at work to make the children obedient and simple and noble. Joy and sorrow are servants in God's nursery; pain and delight, ecstasy and despair, minister in it; but amongst them there is none more marvellous in its potency than that mingling of all pains and pleasures to which we specially give the name of Love.

(ML, 198)

502. He is utterly true and good to us, nor shall anything withstand His will.

(SI, 22)

503. Nor will God force any door to enter in. He may send a tempest about the house; the wind of His admonishment may burst doors and windows, yea, shake the house to its foundations; but not then, not so, will He enter. The door must be opened by the willing hand, ere the foot of Love will cross the threshold. He watches to see the door move from within. Every tempest is but an assault in the siege of love. The terror of God is but the other side of His love; it is love outside the house, that would be inside—love that knows the house is no house, only a place, until it enter— no home, but a tent, until the Eternal dwell there.

(SII, 56–57)

504. God must wait with His own patience—wait long for the child of His love to learn that her very sorrow came of His dearest affection. Who wants such affection as that? says the unloving. No one, I answer; but everyone who comes to know it, glorifies it as the only love that ever could satisfy his being.

(PF, 275)

505. In one word, God is Love. Love is the deepest depth, the essence of His nature, at the root of all his being. . . . If God would not punish sin, or if He did it for anything but love, He would not be the Father of Jesus Christ, the God who works as Jesus wrought.

(SIII, 8–9)

506. Because God is so altogether alien to wrong, because it is to Him a heart-pain and trouble that one of His little ones should do the evil thing, there is, I believe, no extreme of suffering to which, for the sake of destroying the evil thing in them, He would not subject them. A man might flatter, or bribe, or coax a tyrant; but there is no refuge from the love of God; that love will, for very love, insist upon the uttermost farthing.

(SIII, 131)

507. It is no pleasure to God, as it so often is to us, to see the wicked suffer. To regard any suffering with satisfaction, save it be sympathetically with its curative quality, comes of evil, is inhuman because undivine, is a thing God is incapable of.

(SIII, 131)

508. For the love of Christ is an awful thing. There is nothing in that which goes half way, or which makes exception. The Son of God loves so utterly that He will have His children clean, and if hurt and sorrow, pain and torture, will do to deliver any one of them from the horrible thing . . . the loving Christ, though it hurts Him all the time, and though He feels every sting Himself, will do it.

(GW, 125)

509. The one secret of life and development, is not to devise and plan, but to fall in with the forces at work—to do every moment's duty aright—that being the part in the process allotted to us; and let come . . . what the eternal Thought wills for each of us, has intended in each of us from the first. If men would but believe that they are in process of creation, and consent to be made—let the Maker handle them as the potter his clay, yielding themselves in respondent motion and submissive hopeful action with the turning of His wheel, they would ere long find themselves able to welcome every pressure of the hand upon them, even when it was felt in pain, and sometimes not only to believe but to recognise the divine end in view, the bringing of a son into glory; whereas, behaving like children who struggle and scream while their mother washes and dresses them, they find they have to be washed and dressed, notwithstanding, and with the more discomfort; they may even have to find themselves set half naked and but half dried in a corner, to come to their right minds, and ask to be finished.

(SG, 309)

510. The whole trouble is that we won't let God help us.

(ML, 114)

511. We are so full of ourselves, and feel so grand, that we should never come to know what poor creatures we are, never begin to do better, but for the knock-down blows that the loving God gives us. We do not like them, but He does not spare us for that.

(RS, 152)

512. "How can I help doubting that there is a loving God when I see so much suffering, oppression, and cruelty in the world? If there were such a being as you say, would He permit the horrible things we hear of on every hand?"...

"If ease and comfort, and the pleasures of animal and intellectual being, were the best things to be had, as they are the only things most people desire, then that maker who did not care that his creatures should possess or were deprived of such, could not be a good God. But if the need with the lack of such things should be the means, the only means of their gaining something in its very nature so much better that—"

"But," interrupted Clementina, "if they don't care about anything better—if they are content as they are?"

"Should He then who called them into existence be limited in His further intents for the perfection of their creation by their notions concerning themselves who cannot add to their life one cubit?—such notions being often consciously dishonest? If He knows them worthless without something that He can give, shall He withhold His hand because they do not care that He should stretch it forth? Should a child not be taught to ride because he is content to run on foot."

(ML, 187–89)

513. Believe it is not by a little only that the heart of the universe is tenderer, more loving, more just and fair, than yours or mine.

(HG, 212)

514. I well remember feeling as a child that I did not care for God to love me if He did not love everybody: the kind of love I needed was love essential to my nature ... the love

therefore that all men needed, the love that belonged to their nature as the children of the Father, a love He could not give me except He gave it to all men.

(WW, 37)

515. "But aunt would say, if she knew, that, dying as she did, Emmeline could not be saved."

"Some people may have to be a good deal astonished as to what can and cannot be," returned the curate. "But never mind what people say: make your appeal to the Savior of men about whatever troubles you. Cry to the faithful Creator, His Father. To be a faithful Creator needs a might of truth and loving kindness of which our narrow minds can ill conceive. Ask much of God, my boy, and be very humble and very hoping."

(TW, 429)

516. (A young lady's reflection on the condition of her father after his death.)

She pondered much about her father, and would find herself praying for him, careless of what she had been taught. She could not blind herself to what she knew. He had not been a bad man as men count badness, but could she in common sense think him a glorified saint, singing in white robes? The polite, kind old man! her own father!— could she, on the other hand, believe him in flames forever? If so, what a religion was that which required her to believe it, and at the same time to rejoice in the Lord always!

(E, 287)

517. (A fragment of conversation.)

"God *will* have His creatures good. They cannot escape Him."

"Then a man may put off repentance as long as he pleases."

"Certainly he may—at least as long as he can—but it is a fearful thing to try issues with God."

(E, 98–99)

518. (The young hero of the novel explains to his grandmother what he will do if he gets to heaven and sits down at a table with the Lord and the saints.)

Well, if I get there, the very first night I sit down with the rest of them, I'm going to rise up and say—that is if the Master at the head of the table doesn't bid me to sit down—and say: "Brothers and sisters, all of you, listen to me for one minute; and Oh Lord! if I speak wrongly, just take the speech from me, and I'll sit down dumb and rebuked. We're all here by grace and not by merit, save His, as you all know better than I can tell you, for you have been here longer than I have. But it's just tugging and tearing at my heart to think of them that are down there. . . . Now we have no merit and they have no merit, and why are we here and them there? But we're washed clean and innocent now; and now, when there's no blame on us, it seems to me that we might bear some of the sins of them that have too many. I call upon each one of you who has a friend or a neighbor down yonder, to rise up without eating another bite until we go up together to the foot of the throne, and pray the Lord to let us go and do as the Master did before us, and bear their griefs, and carry their sorrows down in hell; so that it may be that they repent and get remission of their sins, and come up here with us at long last, and sit down with us at this table, all through the merits of our Savior Jesus Christ, at the head of the table there. Amen.

(RF*, 96)

519. (A young girl who fears she has hurt rather than helped someone is comforted by her spiritual adviser.)

She feared at times that she had done him evil rather than good by pressing upon him a duty she had not persuaded him to perform. She spoke of this to Andrew, but he answered decisively.

"If you believed you ought to speak to him and have discovered no wrong motive, you must not trouble yourself

---

*Indicates translation of Scottish dialect into English.

about the result. That may be a thousand years off yet. You may have sent him into a hotter purgatory, and at the same time made it shorter for him. We know nothing but that God is righteous."

(E, 184–85)

520. (A description of a system of theology common in MacDonald's boyhood community, which he rejects.)

In such a system, hell is invariably the deepest truth, and the love of God is not so deep as hell. . . . often as a thought of religious duty arose in [Robert Falconer's] mind it appeared in the form of escaping hell. . . . And yet God made him. He must believe that. And he must believe too that God was just, awfully just, punishing with fearful pains those who did not go through a certain process of mind which it was utterly impossible they should go through without a help which He would give to some and withhold from others. . . . And this God they said was love. It was logically absurd, of course, yet, thank God. They did say that God was love; and many of them succeeded in believing it, too. . . . Still the [belief in hell] was the [belief] they brought chiefly to bear upon their children. This mortar, probably they thought, threw the shell straighter than any other of the field pieces of the church militant.

(RF, 90)

521. That a being able to make another self-conscious being distinct from himself, should be able also to set right whatever that being could set wrong seems to me to follow of simple necessity. He might even, should that be fit, put the man himself in the way of making up for what he had done, or at least put it in his power to ask and receive a forgiveness that would set all right between him and the person wronged. One of the painful things in the dogma of the endless loss of the wicked is that it leaves no room for the righteous to make up to them for the wrongs they did them in this life. For the righteous do the wicked far more wrong than they think—the righteous being all the time, in

reality, the wealthy, and the wicked the poor. But it is a blessed word, that there are first that shall be last, and last that shall be first. . . . Is there not the might of love, and all eternity for it to work in, to set things right?

(TW, 309)

522. Heartily He loves you, heartily He hates the evil in you—so heartily that He will even cast you into the fire to burn you clean. By making you clean He will give you rest.

(TW, 342)

523. (An old woman's reflection on God.)

I am old, therefore dare to say that I expect more and better and higher and lovelier things than I have ever had. I am not going home to say—"Father, I have imagined more beautiful things than Thou art able to make true! They were so good that Thou Thyself art not good enough to will them, or not strong enough to make them. Thou couldst but make Thy creature dream of them, because Thou canst but dream of them Thyself." Nay, Nay! In the faith of Him to whom the Father shows all things He does, I expect lovelier gifts than I ever have, ever shall be able to dream of asleep, or imagine awake.

(FS, 56–57)

524. When shall a man dare to say that God has done all He can?

(RF, 515)

TWELVE

 POETRY

525. Keep me from wrath, let it seem ever so right:
My wrath will never work Thy righteousness.
Up, up the hill, to the whiter than snow-shine,
Help me to climb, and dwell in pardon's light.
I must be pure as Thou, or ever less
Than Thy design of me—therefore incline
My heart to take men's wrongs as Thou tak'st mine.
(DS, 22)

526. Lord, in Thy Spirit's hurricane, I pray,
Strip my soul naked—dress it then Thy way.
Change for me all my rags to cloth of gold.
Who would not poverty for riches yield?
A hovel sell to buy a treasure-field?
Who would a mess of porridge careful hold
Against the universe's birthright old?
(DS, 23)

527. Through all the fog, through all earth's wintry sighs,
I scent Thy spring, I feel the eternal air,
Warm, soft, and dewy, filled with flowery eyes,

And gentle, murmuring motions everywhere—
Of life in heart, and tree, and brook, and moss;
Thy breath wakes beauty, love, and bliss, and prayer,
And strength to hang with nails upon Thy cross.

(DS, 49)

528. Oh, make my anger pure—let no worst wrong
Rouse in me the old niggard selfishness.
Give me Thine indignation—which is love
Turned on the evil that would part love's throng;
Thy anger scathes because it needs must bless,
Gathering into union calm and strong
All things on earth, and under, and above.

(DS, 67)

529. Lord, loosen in me the hold of visible things;
Help me to walk by faith and not by sight;
I would, through thickest veils and coverings,
See into the chambers of the living light.
Lord, in the land of things that swell and seem,
Help me to walk by the other light supreme,
Which shows Thy facts behind man's vaguely hinting
     dream.

(DS, 99)

530. Sometimes it seems pure natural to trust,
And trust right largely, grandly, infinitely,
Daring the splendor of the giver's part;
At other times, the whole earth is but dust,
The sky is dust, yea, dust the human heart;
Then art Thou nowhere, there is no room for Thee
In the great dust-heap of eternity....

I know at least which is the better mood.
When on a heap of cares I sit and brood,
Like Job upon his ashes, sorely vext,
I feel a lower thing than when I stood
The world's true heir, fearless as, on its stalk,

A lily meeting Jesus in his walk:
I am not all mood—I can judge betwixt.

(DS, 89–91)

531. NOONTIDE HYMN
    I love Thy skies, Thy sunny mists,
      Thy fields, Thy mountains hoar,
    Thy wind that bloweth where it lists—
      Thy will, I love it more.

    I love Thy hidden truth to seek
      All round, in sea, on shore;
    The arts whereby like gods we speak—
      Thy will to me is more.

    I love Thy men and women, Lord,
      The children round Thy door;
    Calm thoughts that inward strength afford—
      Thy will than these is more.

    But when Thy will my life doth hold
      Thine to the very core,
    The world, which that same will doth mould,
      I love, then, ten times more!

(PI, 319)

532. In Thee lies hid my unknown heart,
      In Thee my perfect mind;
    In all my joys, my Lord, Thou art
      The deeper joy behind.

(PI, 381)

533. What profits it to reason high
      And in hard questions court dispute,
    When thou dost lack humility,
      Displeasing God at very root!

    The eye with seeing is not filled,

The ear with hearing not at rest;
Desire with having is not stilled;
  With human praise no heart is blest.

Vanity, then, of vanities
  All things for which men grasp and grope!
The precious things in heavenly eyes
  Are love, and truth, and trust, and hope.

                                        (PI, 436)

534. (In the first part of the following poem Jesus comes to
a monk at prayer. Then the monk must choose between
duty and the desire to stay with Jesus.)

With sudden clang the convent bell
  Told him the poor did wait
His hand to give the daily bread
  Doled at the convent-gate.

Then Love rose in him passionate,
  And with Duty wrestled strong;
And the bell kept calling all the time
  With merciless iron tongue.

The Master stood and looked at him
  He rose up with a sigh:
"He will be gone when I come back
  I go to Him by and by!"

He chid his heart, he fed the poor
  All at the convent-gate;
Then with slow-dragging feet went back
  To his cell so desolate:

His heart bereaved by duty done,
  He had sore need of prayer!
Oh, sad he lifted the latch!—and, lo,
  The Master standing there!

He said, "My poor had not to stand
   Wearily at thy gate:
For him who feeds the shepherd's sheep
   The shepherd will stand and wait."

                                  (PII, 77–78)

535. THE GIVER

To give a thing and take again
Is counted meanness among men;
To take away what once is given
Cannot then be the way of heaven!

But human hearts are crumbly stuff,
And never, never love enough,
Therefore God takes and, with a smile,
Puts our best things away a while.

Thereon some weep, some rave, some scorn,
Some wish they never had been born;
Some humble grow at last and still,
And then God gives them what they will.

                                  (PII, 128)

536. LOVE IS STRENGTH

Love alone is great in might,
Makes the heavy burden light,
Smooths rough ways to weary feet,
Makes the bitter morsel sweet:
   Love alone is strength!

Might that is not born of Love
Is not Might born from above,
Has its birthplace down below
Where they neither reap nor sow;
   Love alone is strength!

Love is stronger than all force,
Is its own eternal source;

Might is always in decay,
Love grows fresher every day:
  Love alone is strength!

Little ones, no ill can chance;
Fear ye not, but sing and dance;
Though the high-heaved heaven should fall
God is plenty for us all:
  God is Love and Strength!

                                        (PII, 130–31)

537. He cares for you, whether you laugh or cry,
     Cares whether your mother smile or sigh.
     How He cares for so many, I do not know,
     But it would be too strange if He did not so—
     Dreadful and dreary for even a fly!
     So I cannot wait for the *how* and *why,*
     But believe that all things are gathered and nursed
     In the love of Him whose love went first
     And made this world—like a huge great nest
     For a hen to sit on with feathery breast.

                                        (PII, 145–46)

538. The man who was lord of fate,
         Born in an ox's stall,
     Was great because He was much too great
         To care about greatness at all.

     Ever and only He sought
         The will of His Father good;
     Never of what was high He thought,
         But of what His Father would.

     You long to be great; you try;
         You feel yourself smaller still;
     In the name of God let ambition die;
         Let Him make you what He will.

Who does the truth, is one
  With the living Truth above;
Be God's obedient little son,
  Let ambition die in love.

(PII, 178)

(The remaining poems are from a collection entitled "A Threefold Cord." MacDonald selected poems for the collection from his own, his brother's, and a friend's works. The poems below may or may not have been written by him but, in any case, they express his thoughts.)

539. COME TO ME
  Come to me, come to me, O my God;
    Come to me everywhere!
  Let the trees mean Thee, and the grassy sod,
    And the water and the air!

  For Thou art so far that I often doubt,
    As on every side I stare,
  Searching within, and looking without,
    If Thou canst be anywhere.

  How did men find Thee in days of old?
    How did they grow so sure?
  They fought in Thy name, they were glad and bold,
    They suffered, and kept themselves pure!

  But now they say—neither above the sphere
    Nor down in the heart of man,
  But solely in fancy, ambition, and fear
    The thought of Thee began.

  If only that perfect tale were true
    Which ages have not made old,
  Which of endless many makes one anew,
    And simplicity manifold!

But *He* taught that they who did His word
  The truth of it sure would know:
I will try to do it: if He be Lord
  Again the old faith will glow;

Again the old spirit-wind will blow
  That He promised to their prayer;
And obeying the Son, I too shall know
  His Father everywhere.

(PII, 263–64)

540. RONDEL
  I do not know Thy final will,
    It is too good for me to know:
    Thou willest that I mercy show,
  That I take heed and do no ill,
  That I the needy warm and fill,
    Nor stones at any sinner throw;
  But I know not Thy final will—
    It is too good for me to know.

  I know Thy love unspeakable—
    For love's sake able to send woe!
    To find Thine own Thou lost didst go,
  And wouldst for men Thy blood yet spill!—
  How should I know Thy final will,
    Godwise too good for me to know!

(PII, 336)

BIBLIOGRAPHY

The following bibliography is not complete, but is meant to give an idea of the extent of MacDonald's writing and to indicate what is currently available. If there is a publisher listed in parentheses after the title, it means that it is currently in print. If an editor is given, it means that the original has been condensed. Most of the novels are now available in condensed form. Only the editor's initials are given. DH and EH denote Dan Hamilton and Elizabeth Hamilton, whose books are published by Victor Books. MP denotes Michael Phillips, published by Bethany House Publishers. EY denotes Elizabeth Yates, published by Schocken. RH denotes Rolland Hein, published by Shaw. The books of sermons published by Flynn are paperback facsimile reprints in a limited edition. The address is J. Joseph Flynn, P.O. Box 3855, South Pasadena, CA 91030. Michael Phillips is planning to publish most of MacDonald's works in hardback (limited editions). In order to find out what is currently available, write to Sunrise Books Publishers, 1707 E St., Eureka, CA 95501.

It is not easy to categorize all of MacDonald's works. For example, *The Portent* could be classified as fantasy rather than as a novel; and some of the novels e.g., *A Rough Shaking,* were written for young readers. However, I believe that everything he wrote is profitable reading for adults. In any case, I have put his work in six categories: Novels, Fairy Tales and Short Stories, Fantasy, Poetry, Sermons, and Literary Essays. Also included, is a list of anthologies and biographies that are currently in print.

Novels
Adela Cathcart
Alec Forbes of Howglen (The Maiden's Bequest, ed. MP)
Annals of a Quiet Neighborhood (A Quiet Neighborhood, ed. DH)
David Elginbrod (The Tutor's First Love, ed. MP)
Donal Grant (The Shepherd's Castle, ed. MP)
The Elect Lady (The Elect Lady, ed. DH) also (The Landlady's Master, ed. MP)
Far Above Rubies
The Flight of the Shadow (Harper and Row)
Guild Court (The Prodigal Apprentice, ed. DH)
Gutta Percha Willie: the Working Genius (The Genius of Willie MacMichael, ed. DH)
Heather and Snow (Heather and Snow, ed. EH)
Home Again (Home Again, ed. DH)
Malcolm (The Fisherman's Lady, ed. MP)
The Marquis of Lossie (The Marquis' Secret, ed. MP)
Mary Marston (The Shopkeeper's Daughter, ed. EH) also (A Daughter's Devotion, ed. MP)
The Portent (Harper and Row, published in complete form but retitled as Lady of the Mansion)
Paul Faber, Surgeon (The Lady's Confession, ed. MP)
Ranald Bannerman's Boyhood (The Boyhood of Ranald Bannerman, ed. DH)
Robert Falconer (The Musician's Quest, ed. MP)
A Rough Shaking (The Wanderings of Clare Skymer, Victor Books)

Saint George and Saint Michael (The Last Castle, ed. DH)
Salted With Fire (The Minister's Restoration, ed. MP)
The Seaboard Parish (The Seaboard Parish, ed. DH)
Sir Gibbie (The Baronet's Song, ed. MP) also (Sir Gibbie, ed. EY)
There and Back (The Baron's Apprenticeship, ed. MP)
Thomas Wingfold, Curate (The Curate's Awakening, ed. MP)
The Vicar's Daughter (The Vicar's Daughter, ed. DH)
Warlock O'Glen Warlock (The Laird's Inheritance, ed. MP)
Weighed and Wanting (On Tangled Paths, ed. DH)
What's Mine's Mine (The Highlander's Last Song, ed. MP)
Wilfred Cumbermede

Fairy Tales and Short Stories
At the Back of the North Wind (Many publishers)
The Christmas Stories of George MacDonald (Cook)
The Complete Fairy Tales of George MacDonald (Schocken)
The Day Boy and the Night Girl (Knopf)
The Fantasy Stories of George MacDonald, 4 volumes (Eerdmans)
The Golden Key (FS & G)
The Light Princess (FS & G) also (Harcourt Brace)
Papa's Story & Other Tales (Bookmaker's Guild)
The Princess and Curdie (Dell)
The Princess and the Goblin (Many publishers)

Fantasy
Lilith (Eerdmans) also (Schocken)
Phantastes (Eerdmans) also (Schocken)

Poetry
Diary of An Old Soul (Augsburg)
Poetical Works, Volumes I and II
Within and Without

Sermons
God's Word to His Children
The Hope of the Gospel (J.J. Flynn)

The Miracles of Our Lord (J.J. Flynn) also (ed. RH)
Unspoken Sermons, Series One (J.J. Flynn)
Unspoken Sermons, Series Two (J.J. Flynn)
Unspoken Sermons, Series Three (J.J. Flynn)

Literary Essays
A Dish of Orts (Folcroft)
England's Antiphon (R. West)

Anthologies
Rolland Hein, ed. *Creation in Christ: Unspoken Sermons* (Shaw Publishers, a collection of sermons)
C.S. Lewis, ed. *George MacDonald: An Anthology* (Macmillan, a devotional, 365 selections)
Warren A. Hutchinson, ed. *Getting to Know Jesus* (Keats Publishing, Inc., a collection of sermons)

Biographies
Greville MacDonald. *George MacDonald and His Wife* (Johnson Reprint Corp., a reprint of the 1924 edition)
Michael R. Phillips. *George MacDonald: Scotland's Beloved Storyteller* (Bethany House Publishers)
William Raeper. *George MacDonald* (Lion Publishing Corp.)
Elizabeth Saintsbury. *George MacDonald: A Short Life* (Canongate)

Subject Index

The numbers in the Subject Index indicate quotation numbers rather than page numbers.